Poet Motion

Berkshire

Edited by Chris Hallam

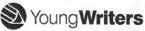 Young**Writers**

First published in Great Britain in 2004 by:
Young Writers
Remus House
Coltsfoot Drive
Peterborough
PE2 9JX
Telephone: 01733 890066
Website: www.youngwriters.co.uk

SB ISBN 1 84460 349 0

Foreword

This year, the Young Writers' 'Poetry In Motion' competition proudly presents a showcase of the best poetic talent selected from over 40,000 up-and-coming writers nationwide.

Young Writers was established in 1991 to promote the reading and writing of poetry within schools and to the youth of today. Our books nurture and inspire confidence in the ability of young writers and provide a snapshot of poems written in schools and at home by budding poets of the future.

The thought effort, imagination and hard work put into each poem impressed us all and the task of selecting poems was a difficult but nevertheless enjoyable experience.

We hope you are as pleased as we are with the final selection and that you and your family continue to be entertained with *Poetry In Motion Berkshire* for many years to come.

Contents

Burnham Upper School

Jóvan Noel (12)	21
Nicky Howells (14)	22
Natasha Barlow (13)	22
Terrina Lake (11)	23
Lily Tidy (13)	23
Ashley Meaney (12)	24
Jack Gifford-Gill (13)	25
Michael Strutton (12)	25
William Marshall (13)	26
Daniel Handley (13)	26
Elizabeth Turner (13)	27
Charlotte Wright (13)	27
Zoe Norcott (13)	28
Joanna Martin (13)	28
Jade Savage (13)	29
Kim Smithies (13)	29
Hayley Dawson (13)	30

Churchmead CE (VA) School

Tayleigh Everest (11)	30
Annie Waddington (13)	31
Shivraj Bhardwaj (11)	31
Daniel Langton (12)	32
Emily Louise Jepson (11)	32
Craig Glennerster (11)	32
Kathryn Butcher (13)	33
Simon Morgan (13)	33
Steffani Kirby (11)	33
Atif Khokhar (12)	34
Luciano Barussi (11)	34
Simran Dosanjh (11)	35
Rebecca Broadhurst (11)	35
Priya Basson	36
Charley Pinkney (11)	37
Matthew Jones (11)	38
Victoria Crawley (12)	38
Aman Tawni (12)	39
Kirsty Williamson (13)	39
Natalie Bailey (13)	40

Sonia Cheema (12) 79
Natalie Thorn (12) 79
Kiranjyot Kaur Nandra (13) 80
Alice Harajda 81
James Brennan (12) 81
Kyle Igbinidion (12) 82
Siân Heatman (12) 82

Dedworth Middle School
Jake Allen (12) 82
Rebecca Beale (11) 83

Easthampstead Park School
Bruce James Fletcher (15) 84

Hurst Lodge School
Tania Firth (13) 85
Caitlin Booth (13) 86
Lauren Cotugno (13) 87
Kristina Spiteri (13) 88
Rebecca Osner (12) 88
Sophie Teeman (13) 89
Rosanna Frett (12) 90
Katia Racov (12) 90
Sophie Chapman (12) 91

Kendrick School
Adina Wass (13) 92
Fiona Hulley (12) 93

Langtree School
Kitty Corbett (12) 94
Anje Wessels (12) 95
Lucy Harley (13) 96

Padworth College
Gwen Sascha Fernandes (17) 97
Natalia Kumar (17) 98

Ranelagh School

Andrew (12)	98
Lianne Moore (13)	99
James Quarrington (12)	99
Robbie Allen (12)	100
Lauren Friend (13)	101
Faye Leppard (13)	102
Jenny White (13)	102
Stephen Boutle (14)	103
Lauren Paris (12)	103
Jessica Blundell (14)	104
Adeeb Burgan (13)	105
Hannah Richards (13)	105
Natasha Ball (14)	106
Hannah Betts (13)	107
Emma-Marie Pugh (14)	108
Katherine Loudoun (13)	108
Hayley Faulkner (13)	109
Alice McGonnell (13)	109
Alex Boundy (12)	110
Ollie Martin (13)	110
Zoë Uffindell (12)	111
Annabelle Shearer (12)	112
Lauren Brown (12)	113
Peter Fellows (12)	114
Kim Harrison (12)	115
Danielle Adams (12)	116
Benjamin Lam (13)	116
Joseph Cole (12)	117
Sam Clothier (13)	117
Alice Pocock (12)	118
Emma Wallace (12)	119
Luke Miller (13)	119
Samantha Burgisser (12)	120
Timothy Rye (12)	120
Rosie Hill (12)	121
Amy Peacock (14)	121
Stephen Newey (13)	122
Jasmin Shearer (14)	122
Zara Mirza (13)	123
Claudia Duncan (13)	123

St Gabriel's School, Newbury

Sandhurst School

The Poems

Food

I like curry
I like sweets
I like fruit
I like ice cream
I like chapatti
I like potato
I like cake
I like jelly
I like crisps
I like lollies
I like cheese
I like strawberries
I like fish
I like chocolate sandwiches.

Shakeela Hussain (15)
Addington Special Needs School

My Favourite Food

I like tomatoes
I like curry
I like pasta
I like sausage
I like chicken
I like crisps
I like cucumber
I like salad
I like pickle
I like chicken curry.

Casey Sinden (14)
Addington Special Needs School

Roast Chicken

Chicken, crisp and golden brown
You get chickens on a farm.
Chickens lay eggs
Chickens have legs
We cook chickens in our oven
Chickens are brown and have feathers
Chickens can be red and yellow.

Adam Jacobs (15)
Addington Special Needs School

Lime And Lemon Time

I think citrus lime would waste my time
because I would hate to find it was involved in crime.

Lemons are juicy and sour
I can eat at least ten in an hour
especially when they're coated in flour
they are also nice when covered in rice.

Nomaan Khan (15)
Addington Special Needs School

Apple

I'm a little apple, green and round,
Here is my stalk, watch me fall and hit the ground.
I'm all yummy and oh so scrummy,
Chop me in half and see my tummy!

Daniel West (14)
Addington Special Needs School

Sausage Sandwich

I like sausage sandwich because it's very nice
with tomatoes in bread.
I like sausage sandwich with crisps.
I like sausage sandwich with bacon but
I also like burgers on my sausage sandwich.
I like fish sandwich.
I like fish fingers in a big sandwich
with fish and chips in, with salt and vinegar.
I like a big plate of pizza.
I like banana in my sandwich because
it's tasty.

Jason Grove (15)
Addington Special Needs School

Bacon Man

Once I had some bacon that could talk,
He was fat and big and could walk.
He was so busy sewing that he was glowing.
Some custard fell on his head
And then he had to go to bed.

Ricky Watkins (14)
Addington Special Needs School

Salads

Salads are green and purple
Little tomatoes are orange
And sweet celery is green and crunchy
Salads are always delicious to eat.

Keeley-Rio Schuite (16)
Addington Special Needs School

Protest Poem

Bombs are whining
Men and women are dying
Treaties are burning
Peace is turning

Depression is appearing
Soldiers are defying
The blood is pouring
While posh people are touring

Weapons are firing
Vehicles are tiring
Children are crying
Citizens are dying

War is causing devastation
Can you help with restoration?
It would be good if you told us your destination
To help this falling nation.

Brendan Rose (14)
Brakenhale School

A Rainy Date

Waiting at the road for a hot date,
It's started to rain, my guy is late.
It's raining cats and dogs, I'm getting very wet,
I've started to shiver, I'm soaked to my bones.
My hair has gone to rats' tails,
I've had enough, I'm going home.

Charlotte Quinton (11)
Brakenhale School

Poem Of Protest

Is this child abuse?

Parents shouting
Children crying
They are hurt
And they are dying.

Parents are mad
The children are sad.
'I hate you kids,'
'Please don't hit me Dad.'

So as I'm in the streets
Parading with my sign
I might ring the police on you
And you can do the time.

Sophie King
Brakenhale School

Animal Cruelty

Killing animals for fashion
Is a hated passion
Giving them pain
Isn't much to gain

Leaving them to die
Yet you still lie
Their lives thrown away
They never get to play

Listen and hear their cry
While birds do not fly
Locked in small spaces
Just look at their sad faces.

Hayley Chappell (13)
Brakenhale School

Untitled

If I do my tie up too tight,
My throat will surely put up a fight.
My shimmering shirt with a golden glow,
Clings on to me and won't let go.
My shoes are loose,
With gaps so big you could hide a moose.
My trousers are large and rather flared,
If the wind picks up my trousers get scared.

Francesca Holland (11)
Brakenhale School

Untitled

You should see me on a night out
My hat is two maracas on a mini stage
My earrings are two rainbows with every colour
My top is Big Ben, ticking away past midnight
My skirt is the roar of a tiger
My boots are crocodile heads waiting to snap at the dance floor
My coat is so long it dangles behind a mile away.

Chloe Cross (12)
Brakenhale School

Untitled

'I'm going to take you home with me and get you out of here.'
From that, my life has been happy evermore,
It just goes to show, that you never know,
What life has got in store.

Lauren Hale (11)
Brakenhale School

Sunsets

Sunsets are pretty,
Sunsets are pink,
Sunsets are red,
Sunsets are purple,
All because of the sun going down.
Silhouettes are black,
Clouds have yellow outlines,
All because of the sun going down.
Water and seas are red,
Water and seas are pink,
Water and seas are purple,
All because of the sun going down.
Sunsets are beautiful,
Sunsets are the best things,
All because of the sun going down.

Lisa-Marie Daborn (11)
Brakenhale School

Gold

Raging, burning now the sun
Walks in the day having fun.
This way and that he burns in fire,
The golden fruit for his desire.
Growing stands a single tree
Catching his rays he shouts in glee!
And golden fish in the water shine
Each one saying, 'His rays are mine.'
In return they give their stream
Into clouds and a sunshine seam.

Joel Forster (11)
Burnham Grammar School

Books, Books And Lord Of The Rings

Sitting in a cosy bed
The story slowly enters my head.
The wind outside whistles and sings
And here I am with 'Lord Of The Rings'.

Tales of hobbits, elves and ents
Outside a cat miaows on a fence.
Frodo, Sam and all the rest
But I like Gimli he's the best.

Saruman and his ten thousand Orcs
Will fight at Helms Deep (which is a fort).
Eyowyn has fallen in love
As her father watches from above.

Eomer has been banished
Merry and Pippin have vanished.
I start to think about the ring
And along come a platoon of Easterlings.

Arwen has made her choice
But now she hears a different voice.
Bilbo is thinking of Bag End
And also Gandalf his dear old friend.

I really, really like this book
I think I'll take another look.

Tess Atkinson (11)
Burnham Grammar School

Loneliness

I wake and start to cry,
But no one is there to wipe my eyes.
I feel the water dripping down my face.
These tears are warm and bitter,
I have felt them so long they seem to fit in place.

I pray leave me be.
For you cannot feel the pain,
Which lurks within me.

The loneliness I feel,
Could be described as surreal.
But the sadness is a reality,
I lead a life full of fatality.

In happiness I wish for peace,
In anger I wish for war.
My complication begins to increase,
A split personality affects me to the core.

I wake and start to cry,
But no one is there to wipe my eyes.
I feel the water dripping down my face.
These tears are warm and bitter,
I have felt them so long they seem to fit in place.

Sukirat Kaur Jandu (16)
Burnham Grammar School

Season Poetry

Spring, Summer, Autumn and Winter sat round a fire,
They thought because it was their children they wanted to inspire,
Spring believed in teaching with slight coldness,
Summer taught using love, warmth and boldness,
Autumn taught using the powers of gold lust
And Winter taught with the threat of harshness,
Now you may be wondering who these children are,
They travel with the seasons; they travel near and far,
Spring's children bring relief from winter months,
March is the first, who saves us from the cold,
April is like the jester from times of old,
May gives us warmth before the summer heat,
Summer's children make it hotter than any month can beat,
June is the first and welcomes us into summer,
July makes it so hot that no one wears a jumper,
August begins to turn the leaves a golden brown,
Autumn's children give the trees a beautiful golden crown,
September begins to cool us after the heat of summer,
October runs with young children over golden leaves;
It could never get glummer,
November decides, before the winter months, to give a final blaze,
Winter's children freeze the world in a last seasonal phase,
December brings joy over Christ's birthday,
January is cold enough to bring about dismay,
February prepares us for the first spring day,
These are the seasons' children that keep the world from disarray.

Dale Thompson (11)
Burnham Grammar School

A Recipe For A Human

Take a healthy body, strong and firm,
Plus a dollop of brains, to help them learn.
Get them bones, to help them stay upright,
But when you put them together, make sure they're not too tight.
Take eight fingers, two thumbs and make sure they don't squeak,
But when you put them on, please don't make them weak.
When you get them organs, make sure you pick the right few,
Although be sure they're not second-hand, but brand new.
Give them teeth, to chomp through beef, a strong bite,
Now add blood, so clean, pure and right.
Now your human's ready to walk, but really you must wait,
They need qualities to help them survive fate.
Take a pinch of pure determination,
Mix it with a tad of blind frustration.
Give them a soul, to make them whole, to make them feel so right,
Give them hope, to help them cope, to know they don't lose sight.
Let them have courage, to get them through life alive
And a bit of luck, to surely help them survive.
Throw in loyalty to help them round the bends,
With these qualities and many more, they will have so many friends.

Danny Hounslow (12)
Burnham Grammar School

Winter Is Here

W inter is here again,
 I t will bring cold ears and sniffling noses,
N o one will escape the flu.
T hough it may be dull,
E veryone will be happy,
R oasting chestnuts on an open fire.

Kirstyn Forward (12)
Burnham Grammar School

The Invisible Friend

I am blinded by the severity of my fright,
I know you're here, I can feel the cold air tonight,
Stop playing games; please show me where you are,
Surely where you are hiding's not that far?

All I wanted was just to have a friend,
For things like secrets, to each other lend,
I wanted to be normal; I didn't want to be left alone,
To do things like talk to one another on the phone.

But instead I endured some devious acts,
When you tried to hurt and talk about me behind my back,
You left me by myself,
Ran off and put me back on the shelf,
Like an unwanted teddy bear
And it's really not very fair.

Why do you despise enough to tell me the wrong place?
Keep me waiting while you laugh, seeing my face,
See an anxious look appear,
As a tear rolls gently down through the fear.

I need to know, so I can progress in my life,
Without feeling like I'm living on a knife,
You lurk behind my darkest nightmare
And release my fear so my heart begins to tear.

I gather up my things and start to leave,
Am I that bad you had to deceive
And lie to purely stand me up?
It's just not funny, now I've had enough.

Emma Scott (16)
Burnham Grammar School

Mr Flea

I once bought a small, brown dog,
His name was Mr Flea.
Soon he choked on an apple core,
It was only half-past three!

I took him to the hospital,
But they told me to go to the vet's.
After I finally got there,
They told me they didn't treat pets!

By now my dog was nearly dead,
So I had to save him alone.
I gave him anaesthetic
And then a chicken bone.

I am happy to say I saved my dog,
He is now alive and well.
But there is still one more problem,
He gives this terrible smell!

I gave him Odour Eaters
And I thought that would work.
But in the end it didn't
And now he's driving a Merc!

By now I have realised,
My dog's not the average pup.
You may say pooch or hound,
Or puppy-dog or mutt.

This is the end of my story,
About a dog named Mr Flea.
He once choked on an apple core,
It was only half-past three!

Michael Bennett (12)
Burnham Grammar School

The Midnight Blues

The moon has been lit,
The stars are bright.
It's blacker than black,
On this midnight night.

The witches on their broomsticks,
Wizards with their wands.
Werewolves howling, *woo-woo,*
Frogs that were princes sitting by the pond.

A ghost starts to play on the piano,
A wolf's on the sax.
A wizard's on the guitar,
It's a time to relax.

The witches start to sing,
They sing the blues.
This is how it goes,
So start tapping your shoes.

I've got the midnight blues
And it's getting me down.
My potions won't work
And it's giving me a frown.

Poor wizards can't do spells,
Werewolves howl.
Frankenstein is moaning,
Tu-whit tu-whoo goes the owl.

Now it's time to pack up,
They leave their instruments put.
'Same time tomorrow?'
And they leave on foot.

Robyn Carlson (12)
Burnham Grammar School

Lost

I'm lost,
I'm alone,
There's no one around me I know.
I'm scared,
Where's home?
I really don't know where to go.

Can't think,
Mind's blank,
My surroundings are merely a blur.
Tears well.
What now?
If only I knew where they were.

It's dark,
Can't see,
Unidentified world swallows me.
So tired . . .
Must sleep,
In bed is where I long to be.

Faint sounds
In the air,
Strain my ears to hear.
Gets louder -
Crunching gravel -
On the road to which I am near.

What's that?
Headlights
Who's in the car? I can't see.
Brakes screech,
Oh my . . .
It's Mum and she's found me!

Sarah Owbridge (12)
Burnham Grammar School

Winds Of Change

Rustling through the trees
People hear but they don't see
The winds of change go blowing through
Blowing through, blowing through

A person speaks against the crowd
We know they're right but we're too proud
To think that they might
Actually be right

Eventually the establishment falls
People answer to the calls
People fight and people fret
Over a war we will forget

How many people must die
And sadden a mother's cry
To stop the wars happening again
Before we shout let's count to ten

This I know will not happen
It will not stop them from attacking
And again the winds go blowing
Blowing through, blowing through.

Elisabeth Ann Brown (12)
Burnham Grammar School

Tetley

(Dedicated to my dog Tetley - 3.7.87.-17.9.03)

Oh no, you're gone
You're high in the sky
You grew your wings
And said goodbye.

You're not dead
No, not really
To you
I'm just being silly.

You're saying, 'Stop it!
Stop the bother.'
But my boy, I can't
To me, you're my brother.

But now you're happy
So I must be too
We'll always be together
No matter what we go through.

You left me a message
'I'll always be with you.'
Now I have a message
'Remember me and I'll always remember you.'

Emily Cheshire (12)
Burnham Grammar School

The World At War

The world, United States, awaiting the next decision.
But to me, how can it be hard
to go to war or not to go to war?

Months, weeks, just to decide one way or another.
Small children cry, they miss their brothers.
But what happens to that poor mother, who's watched her son
or daughter leave the family just, so more lives can be lost?

The decision may take as long as the winter frost.
Nieces write adoring letters to uncles whom they miss, but, what for?
He shouldn't be out there, having two young daughters,
they don't understand.
Their lives seem so grand.
'Dad's on a trip,' they all tell their friends.

But they do not understand, his life is in God's hands.
Life is not grand for the wife who's alone, twisting and turning
beside an empty pillow.
She understands, but does not want to live as a widow,
once a non-believer, God now she accepts.

'He is the one,' she explains,
prays for her husband out on the plains, he's in the front line,
while the public drink wine and laugh and love to play games.

A few days later, a plane crashes, it's his squadron. Poor
wife alone weeping, is it him? She daren't look
outside for the black Navy car.
Waiting, watching, goes to the bar, drinks herself silly,
then a call, 'Please, is it him?' She turns the lights down dim.
'God bless,' she says, folding her wedding dress.
Then another call, it's him, thank God. Yet he cries,
'My mates have died.' She cries.
He cries, they smile for a while, back to work,
She looks out, yes, there's a Merc
Outside poor Sue's house,
Poor little mouse.
Well, what can you do when war is about?

Jessica Rees (12)
Burnham Grammar School

Warm Summer Night

Warm summer night, all alone,
Dewy grass between my toes,
Blowing breeze,
Cool on my face,
A golden path ahead,
That I must tread,
A voice in my ear,
Dancing lights before my eyes,
A whisper comes to my lips -
'Come closer, come closer,'
'Follow, follow,' comes a sing-song voice,
'Follow, follow, follow,'
Down the golden path I tread,
Plants lean towards me, flowers aglow,
With a breeze behind my back
And dew between my toes,
I glide across the ground,
To reach towards the light,
Enticing, enticing,
I reach and touch the orb,
The glowing, bobbing orb,
She appears in a flash of light,
A green angel, so radiant,
Robes of silk draped over her body,
Her fair complexion moves closer, closer,
Her emerald eyes so calming, so calm,
Her lips come to kiss me on the forehead,
The touch is so light as blackness encloses,
The feeling still lingers, still lingers as I lie in my bed.

Amy Wilkinson (11)
Burnham Grammar School

What Are You?

A lion in a cage
Paces aimlessly,
The grass asks, 'What are you?'
The lion replies, 'I know not.'

A parrot in an aviary,
Stationary, in despair,
The bars ask, 'What are you?'
The parrot replies, 'I know not.'

A fish in a tank,
Swimming idly,
The pebbles ask, 'What are you?'
The fish replies, 'I know not.'

A lion in the savannah,
Stalking happily,
The grass asks, 'What are you?'
The lion replies, 'I am free.'

A parrot in the sky,
Gliding gleefully,
The sky asks, 'What are you?'
The parrot replies, 'I am unchained.'

A fish in the ocean,
Swimming joyfully,
The water asks, 'What are you?'
The fish replies, 'I am liberated.'

Kushraj Cheema (13)
Burnham Grammar School

She Made A Difference

Sitting in the classroom with people throwing rubbers,
spitting paper through pens, hiding in the cupboards,
eating chips, eating burgers,
eating loads of rubbish,
then hear this, it will be yuck,
sticking gum under tables.
Pulling hair, snagging clothes, fighting one another,
'Fight, fight, fight,' they all shout,
then there's a bit of bother.

Here she comes with whip in hand,
storming towards the door.
Her nasty looks, her leather boots,
her pile of great big books.

We sit down quickly and go into silence
before she opens the door.
We tuck in our shirts and do up our ties
and put our feet firmly on the floor.

Amie Barnard (11)
Burnham Grammar School

Predator

I will haunt like the fierce wolf.
He prowls upon the deep dark woods.
What would he do?
He was as angry as the beast of the underworld.
He leaps into the air like a soaring eagle
His bold chest sticks up as a lion.
He is proud and he caught his prey.
That prey is the entire you.

Jóvan Noel (12)
Burnham Upper School

And Sure Enough

He was sitting down in the trench
Among the rats and terrible stench
He heard the screams of the dead
The voices lingered in his head.

He heard the whistle and up he jumped
Over the ledge his legs just pumped
The men around him dropped like flies
And still he heard the screams and cries.

The bullets whizzed past his head
And pretty soon he would be dead
He wouldn't make it to their lines
He had to run through the mines.

He counted to three and carried on
But all the other men had gone
He stopped and sat in the field
And looked at who the enemy killed
Then a single round hit his head
And sure enough, he was dead.

Nicky Howells (14)
Burnham Upper School

Silent Diary

Every day hidden away
in a place nobody knows
friends tell me everything
stuff that nobody knows.

When I am closed I am silent
I hold past, present and future
when I open I remind people
of happiness, sadness and anger.

Natasha Barlow (13)
Burnham Upper School

Teachers, We Love You

Teachers, we love you,
For all the kind things you do,
Using your teaching tools and talents,
Keeping everything in balance,
Bringing out the students' very best,
So they will pass the test,
We know for you it is essential,
For them to reach their potential,
In teaching, a teacher goes out of her way,
By bringing in items to aid, day after day,
At times we know there's stress,
Hoping the stress is overshadowed with success,
A teacher has patience unending,
Unselfishly of the time spending,
Teachers, we hope that you know,
That we do care and love you so,
With our love and appreciation,
You are ranked right up with the best in the nation.

Terrina Lake (11)
Burnham Upper School

There's Something In The Room

He's coming towards you,
Making your body shiver and shake,
Your palms are sweaty, your eyes staring into the darkness.
He paused and rested waiting for a movement,
You lay still in your bed unable to move.
He takes your imagination far and away,
Lying there, in the darkness wishing for him to vanish.
He's dressed in all black, staring and staring at you
with his tiger-like eye.
He is coming towards you, every second he's closer,
closer and then . . .

Lily Tidy (13)
Burnham Upper School

Autumn Days

Autumn days, sprinkled leaves
around all the chestnut trees.
The trees moan in the wind
rattling their golden leaves.
Baby animals sleep in trees
trying to keep warm with leaves.
As the birds go to nest
they gather food to eat.
The children gather conkers
from the horse chestnut trees.
When the apples turn ripe
they are eaten from trees.
As people step on leaves
they hear them crunch on the ground.

As the trees are nearly bare
they have no leaves to spare.
The conkers have all gone
broken on the floor.
the leaves have all been raked
into little piles.
All the animals asleep
tucked into leaves.
The apples all rotten
falling off trees.
The grass all dry
from no rain.
All green leaves appear
all over the trees.
The animals awake,
it is the end of autumn.

Ashley Meaney (12)
Burnham Upper School

What Is My Name?

Here he comes to get me
Will he play well today?
I'll have to wait and see
I bet he rang his mates to play.

I hate it when they play on concrete
It puts big scars on my face
They treat me like a bit of meat
Just put me back in my place.

The other day they kicked me
I went into the road
What's that on me? It's just a bee
At least it's not a toad.

Now I'm back in the shed
Laying here all alone
Whilst he's resting on his bed
I feel like a chewed-up bone.

I often feel very rejected
Also tired and alone
It's only when I'm out to play
I'm spoken to more than a phone.

Jack Gifford-Gill (13)
Burnham Upper School

A Haunted Beginning

A silvery full moon has risen
A wolf far off howls
A clock strikes twelve
A tree branch scrapes your window
A floorboard creaks
A figure passes your open door
A noise echoes through your room . . .

Michael Strutton (12)
Burnham Upper School

The Pounding Of The Iron Train

The pounding of his metal teeth as he starts moving
Charging through the night
Twisting, turning like a slivering snake
The burning flame in the body eats wood all night
Always hungry for more
Screeching, hissing as he goes on
He howls without stopping
His bright shining eyes coming closer
With water spewing out of his mouth
His body full of people
The clattering sound of his shining teeth
Then he screams and slows down
With his hissing and howling teeth they stop with a bang
His body empty of people
He screams and starts moving once more
His bright eyes move out of sight into the thick fog
It was as if he had just disappeared.

William Marshall (13)
Burnham Upper School

A TV

He is a big box,
Many people have him and want him.
When you switch him off his screen locks.
Someone comes along.
When you switch him on,
Sometimes he has a song,
Until a programme comes on.

You hear a click
Of the remote control switch
As the TV flicks and flicks.

Daniel Handley (13)
Burnham Upper School

The Death Poem

He creeps and laughs in your dark shadows,
He comes to get old people's souls,
Satan comes for you,
You never know where you'll end up,
He gets you in your sleep,
When his eye is on you he comes to you,
He creeps slowly to your souls,
He reaches out to grab you,
Now you are gone,
He sways with your souls,
He laughs,
There you go in the collection,
Always watch over your shoulder,
Now just make sure it's not your turn next,
Yet.

Elizabeth Turner (13)
Burnham Upper School

Winter

He turns out the light,
he makes dark nights,
I wish he would stay away,
and then we would have a brighter day.

Once he is here it seems forever,
that he comes and brings this dreadful weather,
the rain, the ice, the frost and the snow,
oh when will it be time for him to go?

I cannot wait for this time of year
to hurry up and disappear.
I wonder what he does in the spring,
planning what next Winter will bring?

Charlotte Wright (13)
Burnham Upper School

Changing

His fingers hang from all the rooftops,
With his big white blanket lying across the ground.
When he is near there is no warmth
He takes away the voices of children.

When that one goes the next one appears
She gets all the daffodils dancing in the wind
And the next thing you know new things appear
She gets everyone happy for a fresh new year.

After that everything turns lazy,
He gets all the branches of the willow to droop over the water.
He is nicer with children as now you can hear them again.
She relaxes and leaves things peaceful.

Off jump the conkers of the nearby bald branches
Her breath sweeps the golden, crisp leaves away
She brings chilly weather and it's soon to scare children.
When she has finished the cycle starts again.

Zoe Norcott (13)
Burnham Upper School

Gardener

Green gardens growing healthily,
As the sizzling, sunny summer emerges,
The greedy gardener guzzles Guinness.
Swaying, silently and slowly,
Dressed in dark, dirty dungarees.
He reeks of rotten, rancid rats
That he had killed cruelly and carelessly
Behind the wobbly garden wall.

Joanna Martin (13)
Burnham Upper School

What Is He?

He's always there, never moves out of the same spot.
At times he can look so beautiful
And sometimes you wouldn't take a second look.

You like him or hate him,
He'll help you or annoy you.

He stands saluting
Strong and tall like he's waiting for battle!

He likes to wave at you as the wind blows
Getting old and wrinkly as the days go by
But still standing strong and tall like a building high.

He sometimes gets sad as people climb over him
He often loses his skin as it blows away with the wind.

When it's cold no one wants to know
But when it's hot they come like dogs.

He's often scared he could be turned into paper
But he never gives up
He keeps on fighting as a soldier would.

Jade Savage (13)
Burnham Upper School

A Pen

I come in different shapes and sizes,
I fit in the palm of your hand.
I never sleep I keep on moving,
I have a pointed end.
I need a top up when I'm empty.
I run out all day I can also lay,
You can change my colour,
I munch up paper.

Kim Smithies (13)
Burnham Upper School

Who?

She is there on the 14th February,
She is there on the 25th December,
She's around every day and night,
Awaking when you do.

You find her in red,
Sometimes in pink,
Sometimes they're with chocolate,
Sometimes with flowers.

Sometimes with you,
Sometimes with your friends,
She's there in every room,
She is there when you are at school,
Sometimes at home with you,
Maybe when you're out she is with you.

Maybe with girls,
Maybe with boys,
She's around the corner,
She's there in your heart,

She's with other people in their hearts.

Hayley Dawson (13)
Burnham Upper School

Colours

What is pink? Lipstick is pink.
What is blue? The sea is blue.
What is red? Red is the colour of love
What is orange? An orange is orange.
What is green? The grass is green.
What is white? Cold snow is white.
What is yellow? The sunset is yellow.

Tayleigh Everest (11)
Churchmead CE (VA) School

Beautiful Beast Belle

After an exhausting day at gruesome school,
I sprint as fast as a cheetah,
My shoes panting with the pace, just to see
My best friend, beautiful beast, Belle.

Belle's tail is flying like the rising helicopter,
Her bark louder than the crashing thunder,
Always energetic, wanting an exhilarating trek,
My best friend, beautiful beast, Belle.

Belle yaps for food, waiting for her body fuel,
Her stomach growls, hitting her with agonising blows.
The beast's eyes burn longingly, waiting for her master,
My best friend, beautiful beast, Belle.

The beast is fed and resting silently,
Quiet as the moon shining, star sparkling night,
Wait every hour, minute, second, just for
My best friend, beautiful beast, Belle.

Annie Waddington (13)
Churchmead CE (VA) School

School

On the first day of school,
I didn't know what to do.
I didn't know how to get around,
Every place so strange,
Books lost and found.

So many days have come and gone,
Still counting the remaining days of fun,
How long will my life at school go on?
Will I see my best mate, John?

Teachers always say you'd better study hard,
Get your GCSEs
And a brilliant report card.

Shivraj Bhardwaj (11)
Churchmead CE (VA) School

Poem About Football

What would the world be like without football?
Different players, some big, some small,
Some sturdy and very tall.

Ronaldo's goofy, David James has got weird hair,
David Beckham has lots of flair.
It doesn't matter they're all quite good,
Damn right, with what they're paid, they should.

England, France and even Brazil,
They all play football at free will.
It's fantastic, simply brill!

Daniel Langton (12)
Churchmead CE (VA) School

Blue

What is blue? The sea is blue, glistening in the light,
                The sky is blue with clouds floating by.
What is blue? My eyes are blue,
                The ink I write with is blue.
What is blue? My school shirt is blue.
What is blue? The cold night sky is blue,
                My sadness is blue.

Emily Louise Jepson (11)
Churchmead CE (VA) School

Blue

Blue is the colour of the sea, the sky and the night,
Blue is the colour of sadness and cold feeling,
Blue is the colour of an eye that is as big as a blueberry,
Blue is our school shirts and the pens we write with.

Craig Glennerster (11)
Churchmead CE (VA) School

Autumn To Winter

Autumn starts to expire,
Families huddle around the fire.
Windows covered like a blanket of frost,
Birds on the snowy ground looking lost.
Trees shivering in the unwarmed air,
Wind blows without a care.

Leaves fall as if no might,
Trying to get rid of the unwanted fight.
Branches look really bare,
The sound of life is very rare.

Kathryn Butcher (13)
Churchmead CE (VA) School

The Hurricane

Hurricane spinning at speed of light,
crushing road like cornflakes.

Running around slicing through sky,
picking up cars and throwing like toys down.

It was crazy, had a mind of its own,
but after carnage, it changed its tone.

The air was warm and silent,
the hurricane exploded then quiet again . . .

Simon Morgan (13)
Churchmead CE (VA) School

What Is Purple?

Purple is the sign for riches and warmth,
Purple is the colour of clouds at twilight
Grapes are purple, chewing gum is purple,
The fifth colour of the rainbow is purple.

Steffani Kirby (11)
Churchmead CE (VA) School

What Is . . . ?

What is green?
Green are the leaves growing
On the summer trees.

What is red?
Red is where the tropical
Lychees gaze down the stream.

What is blue?
Blue are the seven seas
Racing around the world.

What is grey?
Grey is the vast, deadly wolf
Lurking in the forest finding its prey.

What is white?
White is the freezing snow
Sticking on the boots.

Atif Khokhar (12)
Churchmead CE (VA) School

Dory

Dory is a purple fish
who eats from an old lost dish.

She is always forgetting things,
loses her phone when it rings.

In and out, chasing bubbles,
trying to forget the troubles.

Dory has many friends in the ocean,
shopping for suntan lotion.

Luciano Barussi (11)
Churchmead CE (VA) School

Teachers

Teachers, teachers, I like teachers,
but mine all look and act
like creatures.

Well . . . Mr Merryman drives a 60's van.
Mrs Macher's blows like crackers.
Mr Pringle loves to jingle,
Mr Hart makes an early start,
Mrs Green is generous and keen,
Mrs Garner is nice but never mean,
Mr Kirby looks like a Furby,
The dinner lady's fat and curvy.

Teachers, teachers always busy,
Teachers, teachers make me dizzy.

Simran Dosanjh (11)
Churchmead CE (VA) School

School

School is boring,
The rain is pouring,
Pupils are bored and snoring,
Teachers are responsible,
7S are writing a fable,
Rubbers jumping on the table.
When the school bell rings,
The class start to sing,
When a rubber goes *ping,*
A bird starts to flap its wing.
The dinner is nice,
When it's chicken and rice,
Playground games,
My turn to roll the dice.

Rebecca Broadhurst (11)
Churchmead CE (VA) School

Summer

In the blazing sun,
I see lots of fun,
Fishing ropes and knots
and beauty spots.
I go to the beach,
run and reach,
I go to the parks
hear laughing and dogs bark.
Friends splash me,
hosepipe, water gun,
but I run till I'm done.

Trees are green, they seem so clean,
as it always has been,
The flowers in the field
with magic powers
gently sway for hours.

The heat makes me
sticky and sweaty,
so I wear
short tops,
squeaky flip-flops.
The wasps spread
their wings,
encircle me with
their buzzing.
Ice cream melting over things.
In the blazing sun, summer is such good fun.

Priya Basson
Churchmead CE (VA) School

Teachers And School

Teachers can be really nasty,
some can be quite nice,
some can be mean and grumpy,
some are hard to find.

When you walk into the classroom,
they shout, *'Why are you late?'*
You get detention after school,
and don't get home till eight.

Teachers are so very nice,
when they give you lots of sweets,
some of them are really weird,
they have quite cheesy feet.

Some people are big bullies,
the teacher tells them off,
the teacher sends them out of class,
then they go off in a strop.

Some of them have grey hair,
some of them are bald,
some of them are really short,
and most of them are tall.

English, maths and science,
football and PE,
and when they are not teaching,
they have a cup of tea.

Charley Pinkney (11)
Churchmead CE (VA) School

There And Back

Past the dusty shops,
People getting off at the stops,
Under the green trees,
Brushing past sweeping leaves.

Carrying weary passengers,
Carrying scrumptious foods,
Carrying treasured luggage,
People with different moods.

Through noisy Glasgow,
To Aberdeen,
Stops slowly at the station,
Lots of queues and waiting trains to be seen.

Back through noisy Glasgow,
Back under the green trees,
Back past the dusty shops,
Red lights, the train stops.

Matthew Jones (11)
Churchmead CE (VA) School

In The Dark

In the dead of night
we all get a fright
thinking about ghosts and goblins.

A shiver runs up my spine
and you know it must be time
for all children to hide.

Light shines through the blind
then you know that everything's fine
because the monster must have fled
so I will climb back into bed
and rest my sleepy head.

Victoria Crawley (12)
Churchmead CE (VA) School

Hurricane

Powerful gusts
Strong winds
The hurricane is a giant of destruction.

They wait its arrival
A scream of horror
Holding on for dear life.

Slices the sky
Cars fly
It sucks up the world like a Hoover.

Homes crumble
Windows shatter
Smashing everything in sight.

People soar
Tears every blade of grass
It laughs maniacally with evil.

No emotions
No mercy
The hurricane is a giant of destruction.

Aman Tawni (12)
Churchmead CE (VA) School

The Battle

Sunlight disappears without a trace,
Meadows turn misty
Sounds of footsteps in the fields,
Coming closer.

Firing arrows,
A dagger to the side
Sweaty bodies fighting for the
Right and wrong.

Until sunlight appears again.

Kirsty Williamson (13)
Churchmead CE (VA) School

A Very Windy Day

Strong winds
Chase the chattering cars
Gusty winds
Creep upon frightened leaves.

Ice-cold noses
Everywhere
Winds blowing
Here and there.

The day takes a turn
Hot to cold
Frozen hands
Destroyed by the cold.

Spirits dead
Too cold to live
The day is gone
But will return.

Natalie Bailey (13)
Churchmead CE (VA) School

Green

Green is for grass,
Green is for trees,
Green is for ivy and
Green is for peas.

Green can be calm, but green can be rough,
It is the sea, colossal and tough.

Green is like eternal peace,
It is like a spring in a desert,
It is a breath of fresh air,
It is deep,
It is infinite.

Dexter Hoogenboom (12)
Churchmead CE (VA) School

Chaos

Razor-sharp winds
Ripped-up trees like rag dolls
Streams of winds
Demolish houses savagely
Tornadoes destroy
Creating more chaos
Turning cars
Sucking up people
Tossing them like little green army models
Tornadoes circled the sea
Ready for battle
As they caused sheets of pressured water
To flood the land
Sea creatures
Battled for their lives
While they fought
With the waves
But everything calmed
The seas died down
The winds settle
And the battle is sealed.

Shaun Henry (14)
Churchmead CE (VA) School

Untitled . . .

A tree blossoms in many different ways
It can spring out with youthful petals or whistling leaves.
It is so beautiful as it stands there all through the winter.
When it warms up into summer
Its bare bones are covered up with flesh-like leaves.
As it stands there swaying to and fro
It gracefully resembles the Statue of Liberty
With a branch as the torch.
She is like a guard at the Tower of London
As she never leaves her post.

Romano E C Henry (13)
Churchmead CE (VA) School

My Bedroom

Pretty patterns on the wall
Lots of dollies short and tall.
Precious secrets I like to keep,
Beneath my pillow when I sleep.
When sometimes on a rainy day,
Lots of friends come to play,
Music, dancing, screaming and shouting,
Jumping, bouncing roundabout.
'Please be quiet' shouts poor Dad
'Too much noise, you're being bad!'
Night has come, friends go home,
Once again, I am alone.
But Mum and Dad and Connie come,
To my room to have more fun.
In the end, it's best to be
Safe with my loving family.

Jennifer Parris (11)
Churchmead CE (VA) School

My Mum!

My mum is fun to be with
Whenever she's about
But when she isn't here
I wish she was about.

My mum is big hearted
Cos she is so very kind
She is simply the best
She deserves a well-earned rest.

You see, my mum goes out to work
From nine until half-past three
But then she cooks evening tea
For everyone including me.

Danielle Miller (11)
Churchmead CE (VA) School

The Ocean Floor

The soul moves softly
Through the calmful sea
Making a seastorm
As she glided across the ocean floor.

Whirl winds whirl
Sandstorms brew
As she strided through
The ocean floor.

Sea creatures scuttle
Sea creatures squirm
Beneath the rocks and pebbles
Upon the ocean floor.

As she reaches the end
She turns to look
She admires her work
And then she goes across the ocean floor.

James Shoulder (12)
Churchmead CE (VA) School

Rain

Drip, drip, drip goes the rain,
As you hear it running down the drain,
The rain falls to the floor,
People running out their door.

The rain gets worse than ever,
Some people say it's only bad weather,
The rain looks like it's stopping,
But it is still dropping.

The sun comes out
And you hear children shout,
'Look at the rainbow,' they say
And that was the end of a rainy day.

Sabrina Piper (12)
Churchmead CE (VA) School

Things I Like

I like football, scoring penalties, it's all fun
Except when you've scored none.

I like cricket best of all
Especially when I bowl.

Spaghetti Bolognese is my favourite dish
Eat it every day, I wish.

I like music with rhythm and beat
Sean Paul's my favourite
Whom I'd like to meet.

Fresh Prince of Bel Air is the best
Will Smith is funny
He beats the rest.

I like it when summer's here
Shorts and T-shirt is all I wear.

Barbecues and eating alfresco
Run out of ice cream
Mum will pop out to Tesco.

Saabir Chaudry (11)
Churchmead CE (VA) School

My Star!

Star, star way up high,
I see you in the dark sky,
You twinkle bright,
In the lonely night,
When you shine,
I know you're mine,
As you sit there in space,
It lightens up my face,
Why do you only come out at night?
Is it because the sun will fight?
You sit there and cry,
As I say goodbye!

Lucinda Sanderson (11)
Churchmead CE (VA) School

Water

Water, water, over there,
Water, water, everywhere,
Trickling off a fragile leaf,
Hummingbird singing sweet,
The feel of drops hitting the ground,
Makes my heart suddenly pound.

For it's music to my ears,
For the water has no fear,
As it dashes down silky slopes,
Like a woven dream appears,
Like a petal falling down,
It twirls and whirls round and round,
For water's over there,
For water's everywhere.

Amrin Kaur Bhatti (11)
Churchmead CE (VA) School

The Sea

The sea crashes into rocks,
White foam over docks,
Drowning voices from people,
Splashing nearby church and its steeple,
Palm trees sway,
As the children play,
Sit on the sand
And listen to the band,
Swimming in the sea,
Cream teas near the quay,
Sand in shoes,
The band sing blues,
The sea is alive,
Deck chairs out till five.

Kerry Andrews (11)
Churchmead CE (VA) School

Wishful Thinking

I wish I was a millionaire, I'd have so many things,
Gold, silver, bronze and those platinum rings.

I wish I owned a sweet shop, right outside my door,
Every day I'd go in and get more and more.

I wish I had a pet lion, in the woods I'd let him . . .
And if burglars came I'd send him out to get 'em.

I wish I had a big house, hopefully a mansion,
Then if it wasn't big enough I'd get an expansion.

I wish I knew the answers to every test I did,
Then all my classmates would think I'm an amazing kid.

I wish I had a bedroom that tidied up itself
Clothes, games, toys, even books on a shelf.

If I had all this money, I would have plenty,
But this ain't gonna happen, I'm not even twenty.

Antony Collins (12)
Churchmead CE (VA) School

Autumn

Autumn days when the wind is blowing,
Leaves and twigs are changing colour,
Frosty mornings and icy breath,
Wrap up warm, ear muffs, half-deaf.

Trees are bare now,
Birds busy searching out food,
Squirrels dance across the damp grass,
Storing nuts before the fast.

Emma Bordessa (12)
Churchmead CE (VA) School

Celebration

Celebration, an excuse for joy,
a chance to throw off the grim façade of real life.

Celebration, an extraordinary, almost inexplicable mixture of all
the emotions and experiences that make your life worth living.
Let yourself go, unchain your fences, your boundaries,
let your world shed the burdens of living for one brief, yet
eternal moment.

Rise above all your past troubles, your past struggle to attain your
goal, pierce the faceless clouds, catch a glimpse of the searing blue,
the eternal freedom and hope its boundless realms offer to the
bewildered spirit, nothing can stop you now.

Let your own and others elation wash over you, wholly flooding every
orifice of the soul, overwhelming your body with such hope, you simply
cannot express the sheer joy running through your veins.

Celebration, life is what you make it,
no one else but you.

Richard Carter (15)
Churchmead CE (VA) School

Autumn Leaves

The leaves are falling, tumbling down,
Will they get so high and make us drown?
Our feet wading, through rustling carpets,
Golden shimmering till the sun sets.

The leaves are coloured and large,
They make a collage,
How long, I wonder, will the leaves stay here?
Autumn a new beginning, I love this time of year.

Mevish Ahmed (11)
Churchmead CE (VA) School

The Fight

Crowds begin to form, waiting for a show,
No going back now,
Punching fearless,
Echoing words travel through the misty air,
Staring and screaming shamefully,
Tears rapidly rolled down his face,
Biting blood burning across their legs,
Cannot plead for help - feeling like a coward,
Enemy cries are mocking,
Footsteps frantically pound like a hammer towards them,
Adults angrily yell - *stop this!*
Silence starts,
Regrets follow.

Chiranjeen Chaggar (13)
Churchmead CE (VA) School

My Feelings

Sometimes I feel so down and out,
I feel I have to shout,
People say I'm depressed,
But really I'm quite stressed.
My family shout at each other and fight,
My mum and stepdad sometimes row through the night,
My dad left when I was five,
All I did was duck and dive,
School was getting hard,
Dad's disappearance left me scarred,
Now I'm getting stronger by the day,
By dealing with things in my own way.

Amii Scanlon (11)
Churchmead CE (VA) School

Smile

Smile when you're happy
Smile when you're sad
Smile when you're angry
Smile when you're glad.

Smile when you're running
Smile when you're walking
But most of all
Smile when you talk.

Smile when you're playing
Smile when you're praying
But most of all
Smile when you want!

Charlotte Stevens (13)
Churchmead CE (VA) School

Books

Books are like little rooms,
You go in and explore,
Whichever one you read,
You learn more and more.

Once in a library,
A whole world opens up to me,
Books are like tombstones for
Famous authors from history.

A book is like a sea of words,
You dive up and you can't get out
Until you've swam to the end.

William Webb (13)
Churchmead CE (VA) School

Forever Friends

Friends are forever, we hope they would stay,
They are always there for you till the end of the day,
When you're in trouble, they are there for you,
Always by your side, whatever you do!
They might ring you up straight after school,
Just think how much they care about you,
When you cry, they make you smile,
Pulling funny faces, that's just how!
Friends are forever, we hope they will stay,
They are always there for you
Till the end of the day.

Satbir Bhullar (13)
Churchmead CE (VA) School

Friends

F is for friendship that should never end
R is for ruining a friendship that can easily mend
I is for important friendship that should always last
E is for endless happiness for present and past
N is for never-ending
D is for dull days that a friend will bring light to
S is for sharing and caring which all friends do.

Khadija Baker (12)
Churchmead CE (VA) School

Paris

P erfect place, Paris
A mazing buildings and statues
R oads are busy, bridges brown with rust
I ncredible towers, famous paintings
S ightseeing a must.

Nikesh Patel (11)
Churchmead CE (VA) School

The Hurricane

Hurricane demon approaches city
Tearing worlds, he attacks our planet
Lightning-fast it chases to infinity
Wind demons control this deadly vacuum
Reporters risk life to catch it on film
It kisses grounds as he rips peace in two
Nowhere sheltered, we confront the hand of death
Monster demon hurricane disappears off planet
Mass evacuation is brought to a halt!

Jamie Poole (13)
Churchmead CE (VA) School

Teachers

Some people like going to school,
Others hate teachers who try to rule,
Teachers are there to teach,
They'll give you the same amount of stationary each,
Sometimes they give out detentions,
Pupils that don't attend will give teachers tension,
I don't understand why teachers like us a lot,
If it was me, I would leave them to rot.

Pavendeep Bansel (12)
Churchmead CE (VA) School

Family And Friends

Friends are very important,
You can share secrets with them,
Family is important too,
They are there to look after you,
They are both there when you need them most,
Through bad and through good,
Always love them with your heart
And you shall never be apart.

Emily Read
Churchmead CE (VA) School

Hello Stranger

Hello stranger
I see your face
I look into your eyes.

Hello stranger
I've seen you before
I've seen the way you smile.

Hello stranger
I see you once again
And I wonder what your name is.

Hello stranger
I search for your face in the crowds
There you are, I've found you.

Hello stranger
Your voice rings in my head
And I see you in my dreams.

Hello stranger
Where are you?
Have you gone?

Hello stranger
You're gone
And it breaks my heart.

Goodbye stranger
I love you.

Siân Richards (12)
Churchmead CE (VA) School

Skateboarding

Skateboarding
With kick-flip kings,
At a skatepark
It's hard-flip Heaven
Rolling along with wheels of fire.

Bailing and getting cut up
Bruising from the head down
Cool kids in cool gear
Skaters on Jackass
Like Bam Margera.

As fast as an Olympic runner
Skateboards roar with anger
Skidding along the ramp
Vert pipe before you
Drop on in!

Skateboarding's cool
Real cool
A sport.

Dwayne Hall (13)
Churchmead CE (VA) School

Hurricane

The wind breezes merrily,
As the gusts barge through,
The colourless clouds gradually drizzle.

Fierce draughts brushed by me,
Hasty winds cover the sun slowly,
Smoky air flutters by violent skies.

Planks of wood glide into the air,
Dust eclipses in the heavens,
While the wind surfs like a roaring car.

Shivani Babuta (12)
Churchmead CE (VA) School

Earthquake

Echoing silence,
Shaking floors,
Buildings fall to their deaths.

Chaos breaks out,
Trembling earth,
Fire rages from gas pipes.

Glass shatters,
Fearful screams,
Separating grounds swallow the above.

Flexible walls,
Crumbling buildings,
Bridges sway and snap.

Aftershocks,
Rebuilding
And all that remains is a memory!

Chantelle Antoniou (12)
Churchmead CE (VA) School

Tidal Wave

Sun shining,
Water splashing,
High upon the sea.

Tidal wave,
Dancing tide,
Reaching higher and higher.

Talking seagulls,
Sparkling pebbles,
Surfs surfing high upon the water.

Tidal wave,
Playful dolphins,
Oceans reach high up as the clouds.

Priyha Mann (12)
Churchmead CE (VA) School

Hurricane

Hurricane, hurricane,
He was shouting at me,
Set me free, let me be.

Hurricane, hurricane,
He was sad,
Which made him mad.

Hurricane, hurricane,
He was damaging things,
I calmed him down by singing.

Hurricane, hurricane,
He settled down,
Then he went out of town.

Hurricane, hurricane,
He closed the door and departed,
Another journey to get started.

Sonya Jalif (12)
Churchmead CE (VA) School

A Flood

Cloudy, dull sky
Fences crumbling
Groaning trees fall.

Unhappy residents
Swimming for help.

Cars moaning and crying
As they drown in the flood!

Power cuts gradually getting worse
Sulking, soggy plants
Get stepped on.

The town's been ruined with this big flood.

Simrandeep Bansi (12)
Churchmead CE (VA) School

Friendship

If I could catch a rainbow
I would do it just for you
And share with you its beauty
On the days you're feeling blue.
If I could build a mountain
You could call your very own
A place to find serenity
A place to be alone.
If I could catch your troubles
I would toss them in the sea
But all these things I'm finding
Are impossible for me.
I cannot catch a rainbow
Or build a mountain fair
But let me be what I know best
A friend that's always there.

Amber Knaggs (13)
Churchmead CE (VA) School

The Hurricane

Winds pick up speed,
As they hurtled across the sky,
Whimpers from animals,
Heard faintly through the rain.
Cars slide uncontrollably off roads,
As the temperature keeps dropping,
Waves crash against shores,
In a rhythmic beat,
Then just as suddenly as it started . . .
It stopped!

Khuliswa Khwela-Browning (12)
Churchmead CE (VA) School

Colour Poetry

What is orange?
Why the sunset,
Like the colour of my basket ball net.

What is pink?
A milkshake is pink,
That I like to drink.

What is red?
My heart,
Which will never fall apart.

What is blue?
The sky,
Where the birds fly by.

What is white?
A swan is white,
Sailing in a beautiful sight.

What is green?
The grass is green,
Where the ants like to crawl in-between.

Sandeep Dhesi (12)
Churchmead CE (VA) School

The Hurricane

The cold north wind
Howled like a lonely wolf.
The rain beat down like small lead pellets,
The hurricane was coming,
People ran inside their houses,
Their windows boarded up,
The hurricane was coming,
Children screaming in the night
Mums held them tight,
The hurricane had finally arrived.

Jasvinder Kaur Nandra (12)
Churchmead CE (VA) School

The Flood

A flood is water everywhere,
Like a huge lake, a small ocean,
Too much, too quick,
Loads of water to spare.

Furniture bobbing past,
Like a boat on the ocean,
People holding on sharply,
Water flowing at the speed of a cheetah,
Tides carry them away,
No time to play.

Then calmer,
Smaller floods,
Not so dangerous,
But even she will create havoc,
She slowly walks away.

As the clear sky appears,
The destroyer runs away,
Sun wakes up
And kisses the sky,
Dampened, sad houses,
Start to dry off,
All is well again,
Until the growing flood returns.

Laura-Ann Hearn (12)
Churchmead CE (VA) School

Leaves

Leaves that smell like autumn
Leaves that crumble in your hands,
When they fall they look like flames in the air,
It looks like the trees are on fire,
I watch my golden friend as she falls off the tree,
Soon it will be my turn.

Charley Balderson (12)
Churchmead CE (VA) School

The Earthquake

Loud noise,
Trembling ground,
Shouting, screaming, increasing more and more.

Explosions take over,
A once peaceful earth,
Time will tell what happens next.

Tragedy and chaos,
God's green earth,
Everything's not what it was like before.

Smoke fills air,
Flames ahead,
A complete warzone, we don't want anymore!

Monish Patel (12)
Churchmead CE (VA) School

The Hurricane

The hurricane, the death chamber,
Racing through the deserted city,
Buildings give in to the cold winds,
Trees collapse to the storm above them.

People flee to find safer lands,
Not looking back at their empty homes,
The ringing silence echoes fast,
The streets once inhabited with joy.

Now the hurricane's been and gone,
Memories crumble in the remains,
Lives are lost in under a blink,
When it will strike again isn't known.

Katy Little (12)
Churchmead CE (VA) School

Countdown!

It's nearly here, the time has come
To count the days for loads of fun
The snow is here, there's no more sun,
So wrap up warm, we're nearly done.

Let's wrap the presents, one by one
The decorations are almost done, leave the presents
Under the tree, not for everybody to see.

Just one more day
The family's here to stay
An early night, get out of sight before
He arrives with a surprise.

Everyone's asleep
Has he left a treat?
Unless we've been bad
Everyone will be sad.

We've counted down
These special days
And now it's here

Christmas Day!

Sophie Davey (13)
Churchmead CE (VA) School

Hurricane Hell

Winds raging
Houses collapsing
Distressed people screaming for help.

Buildings flying
Bulleting rain
Clearing its path like a ghost.

Ploughing through sky
Shattering bricks
Hurricane fades like an exhausted bull!

Adam Kirby (12)
Churchmead CE (VA) School

The Beach

The sun is out, the day is hot,
I'm out of bed and on the beach like a shot.
The feeling of sand under my feet,
Soft and smooth and white as a sheet.
At the shore I paddle in up to my waist,
The salty sea air stinging my face.
It's freezing cold, a thousand
Knives piercing my skin,
I run down to the rocks and jump straight in.
I'm out too far, the waves are going over my head,
I try to paddle my legs
But they're cold and numb and heavy as lead.
The waves have carried me off,
I can't even see the beach,
The rocks are miles away now,
So far out of reach.
My eyes are sore and start to sting,
I try to breathe but let water in.
My brain is drowned,
I get a light feeling in my head,
I fall asleep and
Soon I'm dead.

Jade Hoogenboom (13)
Churchmead CE (VA) School

Chocolate

C adbury's chocolate is Heaven on Earth,
H ot and creamy from the school machine.
O ozing with caramel,
C rispy or chewy, I like them all.
O ut of this world,
L ive to eat chocolate,
A ny time is a good time for chocolate,
T erry's Chocolate Orange, 'it's not Terry's, it's mine'.
E njoy!

Priya Bangar (11)
Churchmead CE (VA) School

Leaves

The leaves are falling,
The trees are blowing in the autumn wind,
Like lost, lonely souls,
The trees are bare,
The branches just do not care,
The leaves are crunchy under my feet,
Brown and withered but wonderful,
Leaves are red as blood,
The piles in the playground,
In their very big mounds.

Michaela Hamblin (12)
Churchmead CE (VA) School

Autumn

Leaves that feel like leather,
Leaves are fun to throw around with friends
And to jump around in,
Leaves that fly through the air,
They are everywhere,
They frolic and tease,
They run and jump,
Bright green, muddy brown or fiery red,
It smells like autumn is in the air.

Chris O'Keeffe (12)
Churchmead CE (VA) School

Laughter

Laughter is golden brown,
Caught by the summer breeze
Left to be cooked as sunshine butter
Eaten to become years of happiness
And it all lives in the heart of you.

Anil Patel (11)
Churchmead CE (VA) School

My Family

My sister wants to go to space,
If she did she would own the place,
She would take over the universe in a fast pace
And she would beat them by punching them in the face.

My mum is always watching Indian soaps,
She sometimes cries and mopes,
Sometimes she laughs so much she chokes,
She will one day stop, I hope.

My dad is always doing work in our shop,
He only serves people who hop,
They go to a fridge to pick up a Panda Pop,
He looks at the person and says 'You flop.'

Sukjinder Hothi (14)
Churchmead CE (VA) School

That's Fate

'No homework again' my teacher said,
'What excuse is it this time,
What measly excuse is it, this time?'
I felt as I was about to cry, the teacher
Won't believe me even if I don't lie.
The truth is it first got blown away,
In the strong winds of May.
Then a dog came and chewed it,
I shouted 'Hey'
My dad came and found me and told me
To go to bed because it was late.
'So now I'm here with my homework Miss,
I guess that's fate!'

Dipti Fatania (12)
Churchmead CE (VA) School

Churchmead

Churchmead is my school
I think it's really cool
It's where I met my best friends
Our friendship will never end.

My favourite subject is art
I will never give up, and always take part
I've had 'artist of the day' twice
I think the teacher is extremely nice.

Drama is also fun
Our group is always the first to be done
We play lots of games
Even games with names.

I don't have any more to say
I hope you enjoyed your day
Churchmead is my school
I think it's really cool!

Kim Woodward (13)
Churchmead CE (VA) School

Bedtime Advice

If tonight when you're in bed
You find it hard to sleep
Then you should think of happy things
And then start counting sheep.

Then very soon, your happy thoughts,
Will gently calm your mind
So when you sleep (through counting sheep)
The sweetest dreams you'll find.

But never! Ever! Think of school
Oh no! For if you do
You may start counting teachers -
And have nightmares all night through!

Lee Sappal (13)
Churchmead CE (VA) School

My Family

My sister is seven,
She thinks she's heaven,
She loves to sing,
But never ring,
Always knock on her door,
If you don't she'll roar,
She loves to get me into big trouble!

My mum has hair,
As brown as a bear,
My mum is very good at computers,
But detests riding scooters,
She loves to watch soaps,
She can cope,
Always make sure your room is tidy!

My dad is the best,
Better than the rest,
He loves to watch the telly
And to fill his belly,
He adores his tea
And he always loses his keys,
When he gets home from work
Make sure his food is on the table!

Amardeep Basra (13)
Churchmead CE (VA) School

Peace . . .

Peace is tranquillity,
Peace is playing with your friends,
Peace is lying in a quiet field,
Peace is chilling out,
Peace is everlasting.

Sophie Jackson (11)
Churchmead CE (VA) School

My First Day In A New School

It wasn't a dream, it was real,
The first day of my new school,
I was feeling cool, I wasn't a fool,
Wearing my new Gucci shoes.

The sun was nice and bright
And I was alright,
We had maths first,
The teacher was dressed in fur.

My hair was in a bun,
I had so much fun,
I made lots of friends,
One called Fred.

Joycelyn Quist (13)
Churchmead CE (VA) School

Owl

You are a predator of the night
With excellent eyesight.

Sitting absolutely still
Waiting to kill.

A powerful beak
And those razor-sharp claws
Watching for movement on the floor.

Your feathers are preened and bright
Shining in the moonlight.

Swooping down to surprise your prey
Before taking to the sky and flying away.

Jack Philp (11)
Churchmead CE (VA) School

The Disgusting Boy

He was here now he's not,
He's round the corner picking his snot.
He never chills,
But he does take pills,
He isn't bad,
He's just mad!
He hasn't got a friend,
Although he does pretend,
When he takes a walk,
He carries a fork,
He is strange,
He goes to the Grange,
It is a school,
That is full of fools,
Here he comes,
Duck!

Shani Baker (11)
Churchmead CE (VA) School

Tidal Wave

The water came down
Everyone around drowned
I stay afloat
On my little boat.

Houses reduced to dust
Cars to a pile of rust
There is nothing left
Except death.

The tidal wave hit
All we could do was sit
And hope for the best
After this day, I'll never rest.

Jason Stephens (14)
Churchmead CE (VA) School

Sitting In My Bed I Heard . . .

Sitting in my bed I heard . . .
The noise of an owl swooping by,
The cry of a cat,
The howl of a wolf
And a hedgehog scurrying by.
Sitting in my bed I heard . . .
The noise of an aircraft flying above,
The beeping of cars,
The ticking of lights
And a rumbling truck.
Sitting in my bed I heard . . .
The thundering sound of the storm,
The pitter-patter of the raindrops,
The cracking sound of hailstones
And the wind whistling by.
Sitting in my bed I heard . . .
Sitting in my bed I heard . . .
The sounds of the night.

Ranwinder Nagra (12)
Churchmead CE (VA) School

Summer

Summer, like a red rose
Starts as a shoot and ends up
As a manky, rotten flower.
Summer, like an airing cupboard,
Its heat never stops.
Summer, opposite from winter,
Side by side with spring and autumn.
Summer, the ugliest of all seasons
With its boiling heat and long, boring days.
When summer ends, everything dies as autumn
Takes the remains away,
Summer, a season of love and happiness there for me and you.

Samuel Gervais (11)
Churchmead CE (VA) School

Summer

Summer has arrived.
Spring has left.
The wait for summer is finished,
People wait no longer to put on their
Bathing suits and go to the beach.

As children move hyperactivity as the sun blazes down,
They don't know that the next time they look in the mirror
They will have a tan.
The children grasp for breath but still wait to hear the tune
Of the ice cream van.

The adults don't have a care in the world
They just relax like they would in a spa.
The children have water fights in their finest outfits.
Even the elderly enjoy the warm breeze of summer
As they take their naps.

All the adults are too busy with relaxing to notice
That children are causing havoc in the world.
The days pass by swiftly like a gentle carousel,
Finally summer leaves and in comes autumn.

Junaid Masood (11)
Churchmead CE (VA) School

Candles

A candle is a lot like a person and his or hers life,
From its birth, when it's lit,
To its death when it goes out,
Waiting and waiting to die away.
The wax represents the person,
The flame represents the life of the person,
The height stands for how long is left of the life,
This poem is supposed to say,
You can look at things so differently,
It's just how you think of looking at it.

Simarjit Raju (12)
Churchmead CE (VA) School

Teeth

They're all at it again,
Warming up,
Ready to bite.

Incisors all warmed up,
Two on the running machine,
Two lifting weights.

Mrs Canine is a pain,
Very strict,
Very sharp too.

Molars getting their teeth in,
Practising eating and attacking,
You can't stop them.

Everyone in position,
Ready, steady . . .
Attack now!

Jeevan Plahe (11)
Churchmead CE (VA) School

Sweets

Sweets are nice and also sour,
I love to eat them for hours and hours,
Hard and soft are all nice,
Jelly beans and mice.

Sweets, sweets, lovely sweets,
Sweets, sweets, wonderful sweets.

Chocolate and white chocolate,
It's all so nice,
I ask my mum for money
And buy sweets, sweets.

Jack Perchard (11)
Churchmead CE (VA) School

Food, Food And More Food

Strawberry, chocolate and vanilla fudge,
They are all flavours that I love,
Dairy ice cream with chocolate sauce,
I would like that for my main course.

I love marshmallows,
I love ice cream,
But I'm not too keen on
The baked beans.

Mangoes, apples and cherries too,
Some for me and some for you,
Munch it, crunch it,
Swallow and eat,
Fruit is much better than cheesy feet.

Carrots, yum,
In my tum,
Broccoli, yuck,
Tastes like muck.

Leah Rhodes & Mercedes Caulton (12)
Churchmead CE (VA) School

My Cousin

My cousin has just had a baby,
I haven't seen her yet,
But soon I'm sure I'll see her baby boy.

My aunty is a grandma,
My aunty's son is an uncle,
Oh deary me.

Now my poem is over,
I just would like to say,
My mum is a great aunty
Each and every day.

Samantha Blakemore (12)
Churchmead CE (VA) School

Billy The Budgie

Billy's my budgie,
Don't you know,
He likes a treat,
Like millet at home.

Billy's my budgie,
Don't you know,
He loves watching TV,
With me though!

Billy's my budgie,
Don't you know,
Come take a look at him,
He's amazing you know!

Amandeep Grewal (12)
Churchmead CE (VA) School

A Very Windy Day!

Outrageous winds
swirling down streets.

Cars swerving
around the fallen trees.

Faces pulled back
by the power of the wind.

Rebellious winds
fly through house windows,
smashing everything in sight.

Blazing breezes,
streets destroyed!

Laura Maunders (13)
Churchmead CE (VA) School

Cricket

As the crowd roars
the batsman steps up!

Running as fast as a cheetah
he released the ball.

In mid-air it spins like a washing machine
and strikes the ground like a herd of bulls.

Ball bounces up and the batsman sets up
coming closer and closer.

At last it's in the right position
oh! What a hit! A six!

Everyone shouts, 'Six!'
and it starts all over again.

Rizwaan Pinjara (13)
Churchmead CE (VA) School

Daydream

I saw my teacher Mrs Machers in Quakers,
Dancing with Mr Kirby,
They seemed quite nervy,
I saw Mrs Green,
She saw me and ran like a runner bean,
Then I saw Mr Merriman dancing on the table,
I think he had broken a brain cable,
Was this true?
Was I feeling blue?
Mrs Machers,
She screamed,
'Detention!'

Rebecca Beldom (11)
Churchmead CE (VA) School

House Of Horrors

The house of horrors lies ahead,
The house deserted by moonlight,
The trees sway violently in the wind,
Trees are bare in their leaves.

The door creaks as I open it,
I enter through the abandoned house,
The lanterns are the only light,
Hung upon the walls.

Portraits stare down,
Their faces all muddled,
There's a slam, I look back,
The door is closed.

I look back to the portraits,
They are gone,
The wind whistles loudly,
I hear voices.

I run for the door,
It flings open,
I sprint outside and run home
And never to go back to the house of horrors.

Jack Holmes (11)
Churchmead CE (VA) School

Summer

Summer is the time of year,
When you want to cheer.

It is a fun and relaxing season,
The sun is the reason.

When the sun is shining bright,
It makes a glistening light.

Everyone enjoying themselves in the sun,
Summer is the season to have fun.

Rabiah Farooq (11)
Churchmead CE (VA) School

Friends

David, Craig and Adam too
We're all friends from Timbuktu,
David's ginger, Craig is brown,
Adam's blond with a very big frown.

Lisa, Emma and Kerry too,
They're all our sisters
And best friends too.
They all hang around
They're all in the same class
But they never ever, ever grass.

Lisa can shout,
Kerry is quiet
And Emma's the one with the smile.

David, Craig, Adam and me
We all go out
As happy as can be
And sometimes we don't know what we talk about.

Now I think this poem has gone round the bend,
So I think I should say, 'The End!'

Ellis Bordessa (13)
Churchmead CE (VA) School

Snow

As I touch the snow and squeeze it in my hands.
It makes my hands numb and makes me shiver inside.
The taste of snow is like the freshest water ever
But it freezes my tongue and makes it numb.
All you can see is white fluff but if it was hot it would spoil the fun
So I prefer it freezing cold.
As the snowfalls, all you can hear is silence
But the village people are overjoyed
That God has blessed us with this lovely snow.

Liam Medhurst (13)
Churchmead CE (VA) School

Mr Kirby

Mr Kirby is our English teacher
He is very good at it
We always listen carefully
And very quietly sit.

He always laughs, I think he's funny
And he always makes us happy.

His hair is neat, he's always polite
And he never ever shouts,
I enjoy my work, I do my best,
He never sends us out.

Lauren Ramasawmy (11)
Churchmead CE (VA) School

English

E nglish is my best subject,
N ever underestimate it.
G lad, I'm very glad I know it,
L ike it or not you must learn it,
I can't believe some people hate it,
S econd language for some people.
H owever it's my first.

Kirstie Banks (13)
Churchmead CE (VA) School

Friend

Flowers will die,
The sun will set,
But you're a friend I won't forget.
Your name is so special
It will never grow old
It's engraved in my heart
With letters of gold.

Natasha Buckland (12)
Churchmead CE (VA) School

My Cat Tilly

Chasing flies, jumping up and down,
Flying high and touching the ground,
But *miaow* she cries, when she's not fed,
There she is under my bed,
Stalking birds up the trees,
Playing in the autumn leaves,
Sometimes she comes home with a gift,
But then it's a mouse, I shift.

Tilly is my best cat,
On my bed, she is probably sat.

Alice Bourne (11)
Churchmead CE (VA) School

Nature

The fire is as hot as lava,
The sun is as bright as floodlights
A match is dropped
The fire spreads as fast as a cheetah after its prey.
A volcano explodes as if it's a predator after prey.
As the sun watches over it the predator wins and the prey is dead
The sun sets and everything is quiet
The fire is out.

Vaheed Iqbal (13)
Churchmead CE (VA) School

The Leaf's Adventure

The leaf was too bored to stay on the tree,
He wanted an adventure on the floor,
To frolic with his friends and family,
When the leaf fell asleep,
The wind blew him across the garden,
The rake was there to tickle him,
But death in the bonfire awaited.

Daniel Janes (13)
Churchmead CE (VA) School

Summer

Summer is the time of fun,
Summer wants to make me run.

Summer gives me a smile,
Summer, it goes on for a mile.

Summer is the best,
Summer beats all of the rest.

Summer you are so bright,
Why aren't you there in the night?

Summer you're there in the sky,
Summer it's time to say goodbye.

Callum Heatman (11)
Churchmead CE (VA) School

Best Friend

B est friend
E xtremely kind
S mile on her face (always)
T he bestest friend ever.

F un to be with
R eally pleasant
I s always there
E very quality a friend has
N ever spiteful
D elightful to be with.

Intikhab Akhtar (13)
Churchmead CE (VA) School

Three Features In The Sky

Clouds float in the blue clear sky
Watching the Earth as they fly.
Cotton wool buds floating around
Watch the shapes as there is no sound

A yellow ball which is caught on fire
Blowing hot air which is hard to desire.
It can burn you if you get too close
But still gives light as it floats.

The moon has turned nocturnal
At night it has become the colonel.
Looking after the world as it rotates
Giving light to every state.

Sonia Cheema (12)
Churchmead CE (VA) School

Colours

The grass is as green as my English book,
The rose is as red as blood,
The shed is as brown as cardboard,
The patio is as grey as the lead in my pencil,
The shrubs are all multicoloured
That is how I like my garden.

The blue in the rainbow is as cold as ice,
The yellow in the rainbow is as bright as the sun ,
The violet in the rainbow is as clean as a white sheet,
The pink in the rainbow is as soft as a baby's bum,
The rainbow is bright, that is how I describe my life.

Natalie Thorn (12)
Churchmead CE (VA) School

Katie Kupp

Beware you children, who tell lies,
You could be in for a great surprise,
Just like naughty Katie Kupp,
Who by a wolf was eaten up.

'There's a wolf in my back garden!'
The people in fright shouted out,
'Pardon?'

The people stopped and started screaming,
Katie stood there happily beaming,
The people rushed to save her,
They looked for the wolf's dirty fur.

The wolf was nowhere to be seen,
The people looked around frightened but keen,
Katie was in fits of laughter,
Oh how the people loathed her.

This happened again and again,
And again and again and again and again,
Until the people could take no more,
Katie stamped her foot on the floor.

But one dreadful, scary night,
Katie slept in shivering fright,
From the wolf she heard a roar,
Upon the wall he scratched his claw.

'There's a wolf,' poor Katie was screaming,
This time you could see she was not beaming.

The wolf slowly climbed up the wall,
Katie prayed that he would fall,
The wolf grabbed Katie and began to eat,
He started munching from her feet.

Kiranjyot Kaur Nandra (13)
Churchmead CE (VA) School

Me, Myself and I

I'm Alice, I'm me,
Eyes as blue as the sea.
Lips as red as a rose.
I have brown hair,
I am noticed anywhere.

I'm not tall as the naked eye may see,
Friends tower over me,
Not skinny, not fat,
I'm me and that's that.

My hair is quite short, as short as me,
I would like to be taller,
That's what I'd want to be.

My smile lights up your face,
Not to my belief, not any time
Nor place.

My temper's like a bomb,
Ready to go at any time,
Tick-tock, tick-tock.

I'm a drama queen, I'm OTT,
I'd come across quite,
Although I know, that's not me.

That's me, all of me,
Not too much, not too less.
I'm me and I like me, I'm the best.

Alice Harajda
Churchmead CE (VA) School

My Limerick

There was a green snake called Drake,
Who got into a fight with a rake,
It swiped off his tail,
The green snake went pale
And that was the end of his tail.

James Brennan (12)
Churchmead CE (VA) School

The Leaf

The leaf was too bored to stay on the tree,
The leaf was free when it fell from the tree,
The leaf wanted an adventure through the air,
It twisted and turned as it fell to the ground,
In the end, it settled with his family.

Kyle Igbinidion (12)
Churchmead CE (VA) School

Alone

You are not alone, not now or forever,
Someone above will always watch you
Until your time will come to meet above
And become one who is there when others are
Alone.

Siân Heatman (12)
Churchmead CE (VA) School

Strange Fruit

The strange fruit tree it does appear
Has dangling fruit twelve times a year.
It has no leaf, no roots, no bud
The rain that makes it grow is blood.
I find this tree has never been
Like other fruit trees all fenced in.
But by the roadside it stands for years
Yet no one steals the fruit I hear.
I've seen this fruit, noted it,
Not put in jam, but in a pit.
Like all bad fruit both far and wide,
It's eaten by the worms inside.

Jake Allen (12)
Dedworth Middle School

Amy's Magic Wand

'It really will work,' said Amy one day,
Just as our teacher was clearing away.
'If I wave this wand and say the right words
That pile of maths books will turn into birds.'

Chalk powdered our hair, ink squirted our faces,
The rulers and pencils began to run races.
Our teacher became a most elegant pig
Waving his trotters and dancing a jig.

I got it for Christmas from my Uncle Stan,
Such an amazing, mysterious man.
He wears a long cloak, a tall, pointed hat,
A wizard of course, no doubt about that.

Our headmaster started to shout
As big erasers were rubbing him out.
Miss Brown grew a beard, Miss Green went red
With the caretaker's mop stuck on her head.

The school went so crazy it gave us a fright
But Amy's uncle made everything right.
Except from one thing, a real disaster,
He could not seem to return our headmaster.

Rebecca Beale (11)
Dedworth Middle School

Dreams

All day I think of you,
All night I dream of you.
When I have thoughts in my head,
They stay with me when I go to bed.
I'll conjure up a dream just for you,
Always hoping I'll be in it too.
The dreams I have are so good,
If only you would see them if you could.

If you'll be with me, we'll go everywhere,
We'll jump from the floor and fly through the air.
Soar through the clouds and up to the moon,
Heaven's there, we'll get there soon.
Take my hand and come with me,
Stand here beneath this tree.
Wait to see the moonlit beams,
And we'll fly up into our dreams.

Every night seems like Heaven,
Until I wake up at seven.
I wait for the hours to go by,
For me to go home and on my bed I lie.
On my bed I then wait,
To find you come home ever so late.
After dinner we both go to bed,
On the pillows we rest our head.
Holding hands palm to palm,
Suddenly fall to sleep in each other's arms.

. . . Into our dream we will fly,
Turn to the world and say goodbye,
For our love will never break,
Because we will never wake . . .

Bruce James Fletcher (15)
Easthampstead Park School

Rescue Me

Rescue me, rescue me
I cry to the squashed flat faces behind the rusty wire mesh
Staring as though I am the world's greatest entertainer
My tricks are trudging along, head down, walking in circles all day long
Bored and boring.
Tell me this. Why does everyone stare at me?

Rescue me, rescue me
I long to stretch my legs, I'm running free as the wind, through fields of
Long, lush, green blades, then I reach a pond, bright blue in colour
I take long sips of such wonderful, delicious tasting water
My heart content
Tell me this. Why can't life be like my imagination?

Rescue me, rescue me
I look around at the reality of my world
Bleak grey concrete surrounded by a muddy, murky, brown moat
Feeding time is but once a day in my dreary existence.
The highlight of the day for me and those continually staring faces
One bony fish is all I get
Tell me this. Why does my world consist of this?

Rescue me, rescue me
The meaning of 'full' has never actually been discovered by me
The phrase 'eternal happiness' is not in my vocabulary
The word 'free' has nothing to do with me
Tell me this. Why does the sentence, 'I am starving, unhappy and
 trapped' have anything to do with me?

Rescue me, rescue me
No one will, there's no joyful end in sight for as long as people pay to
                                                    stare . . .
My destiny will remain here and not elsewhere.

Rescue me, rescue me.
I'll tell you this
The place where I live
They call it a zoo.

Tania Firth (13)
Hurst Lodge School

In Writing There Are . . .

In writing there are no errors
You are never wrong
In writing the new adventures
Are waiting to begin
In writing I feel safe
An invisible wall is laid, so strong it must be impossible
In writing there are smiles
They seem to light up my day
In writing there are tears
That express the things I feel
In writing there are poems
They don't have to rhyme
In writing I can explore
My mind and heart and soul
In writing there are no boundaries
My mind is left to excel
In writing I am free to dream
I never seem to be bored
In writing I find shelter
From things I want to forget
In writing I remember
All the things you didn't
In writing people read
What seems impossible to comprehend
I writing I understand
What I can't always see
In writing I find love
That you seem to have forgotten
In writing I think I feel
What you tried to explain
In writing I feel confused
How could it be all this?
In writing I feel passion
I don't know if you feel it too
In writing I find freedom
In writing I find faith
In writing I find passion

In writing I find something that I don't think I can explain,
I think I understand it, but there is confusion inside me
that I guess I may never really comprehend.
Writing cannot be summed up in a sentence. It cannot be defined.
There are no boundaries. I wish I could call it mine.

Caitlin Booth (13)
Hurst Lodge School

Deep Dark Ocean

I look at the sea and what do I see?
A deep dark ocean
Full of deep dark secrets.

I look at the ocean and what do I see?
A deep dark secret
A sudden fear is in me.

I look at the sea and what do I see?
It's dark and hungry
It's going to take me
To that deep dark secret place that exists beneath me.
The storm has begun in this deep dark ocean
First the whistling, then the heavy wind.
Then the lightning and then the thunder begins.

The rain is heavy and the howling is loud.
The deep dark ocean is crying and proud.

The storm is still mad and angry
And I am worried and scared
For now I know the ocean's deep dark secrets
Are going to take me
Away!

Lauren Cotugno (13)
Hurst Lodge School

The Party Pooper

Parties are so fun for other girls
with their pink dresses and delicate curls
but then there's me, and I'm OK
making fun of the girls on their birthday

They prance around like a rabbit on the run
giggling, smiling and having fun
I smirk and snigger when they do this
parading around as if it's bliss.

I hate the way every girl thinks it's their special day
laughing, playing and acting joyful all day
but I really hate when the birthday cake comes out
and every girl puts on her best fish-like pout

I pull an evil face as they munch their cake
as if they're a duck drinking thirstily from the lake
they all scoff the food from the lunch table
like horses guzzling hay from their stable.

The girls tell their parents, 'The party's been super!'
but that's not for me.
I'm the party pooper.

Kristina Spiteri (13)
Hurst Lodge School

Colours Then Death

You see red, as the anger boils up and bubbles over inside you.
Then blue and you hear someone say, 'Shhhh, be calm!'
There is green in your eyes as you walk back into the world
And yellow as the warm sun fills you with the glory you once had

But then black as you get to night and there it is
Death
Waiting for you.

You see the bright white light as someone steps towards you

Then . . .

Rebecca Osner (12)
Hurst Lodge School

Postcard From The Jungle

Going through the jungle
there are plants everywhere.
The noise of the animals seems
to be somewhere.
The long leaves on the trees
are swooping high.
The day seems to be going by.

As the night draws near all
around me.
I can hear the animals whistling
in the trees.
As I trek through the bushes and
the trees
I can hear something crawling right
behind me
I stay very still hoping it might not be
a monkey, tiger or chimpanzee.

Then suddenly I'm face to face
With a tiny little parrot egg.
I look around. Nothing to see
So I take the egg back with me.

The sun rises high in the sky
Its melting objects going by
Suddenly I hear a cracking
To find that the egg is hatching.

The tiny little bird that I can see starts flying
All around me.
Now I've finished my journey once and
For all.
Can't wait to get home and see you all.

Sophie Teeman (13)
Hurst Lodge School

All Grown Up

The fresh, crisp sound as my foot crunched
Into the freshly fallen snow.
The happy, joyful, playful times
At playing in the snow
Snow angels, snowballs,
And by far the best - snowmen.
The cheerful family walks
I have had in the wood.
The fun and happiness of
Playing with my joyful siblings
The tasty hot chocolate
And our endless fun.
But, now I am all grown up
And my childhood far behind me.

Rosanna Frett (12)
Hurst Lodge School

Air

When I wake up I smell the fresh air
Blowing softly at my hair
Though it slips right past my face
It leaves a cold and loving trace.
Oh, air is like a dream come true
It gives me love, I love it too
Sure, people just think it's for breathing
Though all around us air is weaving.
Spinning round us to and fro
No one knows where it will go.
So don't take advantage of the air.
Give it love and give it care.

Katia Racov (12)
Hurst Lodge School

World War II

The sky is grey, filled with tears from a sobbing cloud
German soldiers give orders out loud

Jews stand nervously in line
World War II started in 1939

Children and adults died on the street
Others starving and had nothing to eat

Millions of Jews murdered and shot
Bodies left on the roadside to rot

Hitler was evil and was around and about
He would put you in camps where there was no way out

A lucky few survived and were fine
But most were dead under the soil and grime

The war went on for five horrific years
Thousand of our brave soldiers died in battles and tears

The war finally ended in 1945
Many thousand no longer alive

Remember the brave people who died for us then,
The women, the children and the men.

Sophie Chapman (12)
Hurst Lodge School

Strawberry Dreams

Strawberry dreams of a far-off place,
Of a silver moon and clouds made of lace.
Strawberry dreams of enchanted kisses,
Of shadowy echoes and haunting reminisces.

Strawberry dreams of a paradise beach,
Of a rippling surface that's just out of reach.
Strawberry dreams of an endless sky,
Of a place where the sun never seems to die.

Strawberry dreams of a broken heart,
Of an exotic love doomed from the start.
Strawberry dreams of a far-off lullaby,
Of a place where you forget what it is to cry.

Strawberry dreams of white golden sand,
Of walking along, hand in hand.
Strawberry dreams of moments long gone,
Of distant conversations like words of a song.

Strawberry dreams of a blood-red sky,
Of looking up and wondering why.
Strawberry dreams of night upon me creeping,
Of being betrayed while peacefully sleeping.

Strawberry dreams of being ripped away,
Of a wonderful, warm strawberry day.
Strawberry dreams of strawberry nights,
When all strawberry wrongs are put to rights.

A light's flicked on,
Strawberry dreams are gone,
All I have is a memory of how the sun once shone.

Adina Wass (13)
Kendrick School

Disabilities

Why do people shout and jeer
And call us funny names?
We're no different on the inside
Just the out.

Why does everyone have to look the same?
Isn't that boring?
What's wrong with a wheelchair, one leg, no thumb?
We're still human.

Why are we named as different
And shunted out?
Why will no one be a friend?
Are they afraid?

Why should we have to feel ashamed
Of what we are?
We're not weird, or mad, or selfish
It's the inside that counts.

Fiona Hulley (12)
Kendrick School

Everything Is Nothing And Nothing Is Everything

Doing nothing in particular,
Not noticing that what we take for granted,
Soon, will be gone,
We misuse them,
In all sorts of ways,
We don't think about them,
How precious they are,
How much we need them,
To enjoy life,
We only have them once,
Some don't have them at all,
We should be grateful for them,
And not waste them away,
On silly things that don't really matter,
We all worry too much,
We've got to let go of all our problems,
Before gravity lets go of us.

Kitty Corbett (12)
Langtree School

The Ladder Of Living

I climb the ladder of living,
It seems so solid and strong.
But it is unforgiving,
It'll collapse with one foot wrong.

Some ladders are 100 feet tall,
Others, one rung high.
This is when people fall,
When fate decides they should die.

Some have a smooth and shiny end,
Others are jagged and black.
This, I'm sure, does depend,
On whether they would go back.

I can see blue sky above,
As I climb the ladder of living.
On my shoulder perches a dove,
The bird of peace starts singing.

Anje Wessels (12)
Langtree School

The River In Motion

Along the river the water flows,
Down the river, down it goes.

Under the trees the river moans
Down the river, down it drones.

All the atmosphere is still,
Through the trees and down the hill.

The water's brown and murky, against the summer's sun
On the grass there're children, playing and having fun.

There're ripples in the water, made by ducks and fish,
Throw in a shiny penny, hope it grants your wish!

The boats are floating gently, down the water's edge,
The newborn baby birds are singing in the hedge.

There's a rainbow in the distance, all colours shining bright,
The sky is blue as blue, not a single cloud in sight.

The old bridge still stands proud and tall,
When you look over, make sure you don't fall.

All the daffodils have come out,
The tulips too without a doubt.

The sight is like an angel sent from above.
The sight is like an angel sent with His love.

Lucy Harley (13)
Langtree School

Child Labourer

When the moon shines high
And the plains of the world lie in slumber
I wake to the threat of a whip.
Here I am in my ragged excuse for rags;
Hoping a breeze would reveal my beloved Orient
But I have nobody there . . .
They lead us like they would unwilling cattle
To that house where monstrous machines
Spit out endless lines of cotton and grease
I stand there, merely an ant in a jungle of rumbles and orders
Taking the thread, I start to roll it;
My eyes fluttering with sleep or rather lack of it.
I could not know what happened
Until I felt his whip lash my bony back.
The pain of a thousand knives threw me to his feet
If only I stayed awake . . .
I slogged till midday.
Hands rough, feet callused from the dirty wooden floor
I had only two consolations;
The young boys I saw in their dirty magical machine, kicking a ball.
We watched when he was away,
Never daring a smile when he was around.
I could play too. I am not much older than twelve.
The second was that I was not alone.
Every evening when we await our tiny rations
We talk about where we will go and what we will do
But what future can we possibly hope to have
For we are tiny nothings in our world like dirt.
We are only the unsung workers for wear.

Gwen Sascha Fernandes (17)
Padworth College

What Love Said . . .

Everything is lost and silent in the stillness of this night,
I cannot but marvel at this amazing sight;
Yet, I wonder how I suddenly see life with such depth;
And when I realised this distance between us;
I just wept.

How did you reach my heart?
How did you get in?
When I think of my present love
I cannot ignore that this is a sin.

A sin so exciting, and so passionate?
I cannot admit that I am lost,
Lost in that gaze,
I don't know where I am,
And all is but . . . a haze.
Help me love, cos I'm lost in this -
This love maze.

I doubt if I can think straight,
I have left the past and entered your mystical gates;
I listened to my heart and not my head -
I just did what love said . . .

Natalia Kumar (17)
Padworth College

The Sun

Gigantic ball of gas and fire,
Floating in the universe,
You never fail to bring us light,
Never-ending gas and light.

Andrew (12)
Ranelagh School

Never-Ending Rain

Looking out my window watching the world go by,
Wondering what went wrong and why you had to lie.
Wipe a tear from my eye, struggling to stay sane,
My heart can't take this pain and never-ending rain.

Raining on me, won't you save me?
Raining on me, baby help me,
Raining on me, down on my knees,
Raining in my heart from the day we had to part.

Looking in the mirror, this girl I used to know,
Swept away with the rain, washed away with the flow.
Now the sun is drying my heart and tears,
I'm so much stronger and proud to have lost these fears.

Raining on me, over and over I tried,
Raining on me, over and over you lied,
Raining on me, over and over you denied,
Raining in my heart all my love for you has died.

Lianne Moore (13)
Ranelagh School

Blood

Blood
Blood everywhere
Blood splattered all over the trampled grass and lacerated corpses
Blood jetting out of the wounds of dying men
Blood on the hands of the men who have slain many a foe
Blood multiplying in size and mass as more men fall.
And still it comes
Blood on trees
Blood on the ground
But then it stops,
And about a tenth of the army that walked on, walked off
With cheers and victory dances.
This is the effect of war.

James Quarrington (12)
Ranelagh School

Betrayal

When I turn my back on you,
What's the first thing that you do?
You swear at me and put me down,
So I will never ever turn around.

I'm not always there to check on you,
To watch and check everything you do,
So everything has got to stop,
The insults, the rumours, the whole lot.

You're telling secrets you swore you'd never tell,
And you're spreading so many rumours as well,
I forget everything we've done,
The smiles, the laughter and all the fun.

I've had enough - it stops right here,
I'm hoping I can live without the fear,
That you'll never ever betray me,
So here it stops, finally.

I can now live my life fine,
Knowing that you'll never cross that line,
But the next time you turn your back on me,
I'll put you down, you'll see.

I'm now giving you the choice,
To stay the hell out of my life,
Or you choose option number two,
Which is where, I forgive you.

Robbie Allen (12)
Ranelagh School

Why?

Why does he keep on hitting me?
Why won't he leave me be?
Why does my mum still love him?
Will there be justice for his sin?

He treats me like I'm awful scum.
Why does he think that's it's so fun?
He bullies me and calls me names,
But this is real, not just a game.

This isn't a story, or something that you read.
A family man, a real dad, is really what I need.
I want to hide or run away, but can't bring myself to leave.
I don't think he's got a soul, or how could he deceive?

I really want to tell someone,
Tell them what he's done,
Instead it's stored inside me,
Wanting to be free.

I want someone to take me, save me from this place,
I want to go, be left alone and never see his face.
I'm feeling so alone, there's no one I can talk to,
There's no one that will understand, just what I have been through.

Right now my heart is aching
And my hands are still shaking.
This has turned into a nightmare, a dream comes to life,
Except that this horrid dream lives on and destroys my life . . .

Lauren Friend (13)
Ranelagh School

Dreams

Cross my fingers, close my eyes,
Hope my dreams won't fade and die,
Deep within my broken heart,
I know we shouldn't be apart.

Love can give and love can take,
Through these hours of heartache,
Thoughts keep running through my head,
Of what's been done and what's been said.

On and on my heart keeps burning,
While I sit here, sad and yearning.
I don't know where I belong,
Why oh why do things go wrong?

Time goes on and passes by,
I promised myself I wouldn't cry,
I'll get through this, I'll move on,
But right now the moment's gone.

Faye Leppard (13)
Ranelagh School

As I Walked Out One Evening

As I walked out one evening,
The sky was ever so black,
With gold glistening eyes,
Looking back at me.

As I walked out one evening,
The leaves were ever so still,
Only the owl was hooting,
Its feathers falling astray.

As I walked out one evening,
Lights flickered off one by one,
People slept in their warm beds,
But still I carried on.

As I walked out one evening.

Jenny White (13)
Ranelagh School

Remember Me When I Go Away

'Remember me when I go away,'
Said the sailor to his bride,
As he boarded the submarine
By the rain-soaked, sad quayside.

She feels the cold air smacking her face,
And a feeling of emptiness,
'He'll be gone for half a year or so
So mine's a life of loneliness.'

But that's one thing he can never have,
In his sub beneath the sea,
'We're all packed in like sardines here,
It's always us and not me.'

But he can never come back,
His grave lies under the sea,
His grieving widow stands alone,
She remembers him on the quay.

Stephen Boutle (14)
Ranelagh School

Leaves

As I see a little leaf
Flutter to the floor
I take a look around me
And see many more

Large and small, brown and green
Shapes and colours to be seen
They are visible everywhere
In the trees and in my hair

When the wind blows
And the branches shake
Down come more
To rest on the floor.

Lauren Paris (12)
Ranelagh School

Gone To Dance With The Dolphins

(For my friend Alex)

Salty waves wash the sand
And all the creatures swim up too
But swimming most silently, softly and smoothly
The dolphin wanders by.

'Come and dance,' it cries
'Come to the water, come and swim'
And as they all go to pet it and dance
One more small dolphin comes swimming up
And cries, 'Remember me, remember me,
Remember me?'

But one small boy sits at the back
For he cannot see, for he is too small
And so the one small dolphin comes swimming up
And calls, 'Come, come, come
And dance with me.'

And so he sets foot into the sea
Into the wet, wet water
And off he goes to dance
To dance in the love of fishes and fins
To dance to dance
To dance forever.

Jessica Blundell (14)
Ranelagh School

Leopards

The leopard is a dangerous animal,
It hunts down what it seeks,
The great leopard is a powerful mammal,
And seldom does it greet.

The leopard is a beautiful creature,
Its fur is spotted black,
The leopard has its own distinctive features,
And knows not to turn back.

The brilliantly speedy leopard stalks,
It prowls along the land,
The leopard is like a fast, enormous hawk,
Its every fast move grand.

The leopard is a dangerous animal,
It hunts down what it seeks,
The great leopard is a powerful mammal,
It just greets what it eats.

Adeeb Burgan (13)
Ranelagh School

Bewitched

At the street corner hunched up,
There sat a little figure,
Their face as white as a newborn pup,
But they also looked no bigger.

I looked and stared long and hard,
They never moved a muscle,
Their arms as stiff as iron bars,
As they heard my crisp packet rustle.

They turned and looked as I strolled on by,
The feeling of guilt inside me
I couldn't feel worse as they muttered a curse
The words that they said bewitched me!

Hannah Richards (13)
Ranelagh School

Our World

False dreams, all false
Everything I've ever known
Secrets and lies
All hidden from my eyes
Hope and despair
I do not care

This world is a lie
It's not for I
All these promises
Of a better world and bliss
Pollution creeps in
And ruins everything.

This world is not our own
Where birds are free
And people are allowed to be
What they want
Without cruel society
Bring them down.

Is this what you want
For future children?
Everyone is equal
And money doesn't rule everything
Love and hope
The foundation for building.

Natasha Ball (14)
Ranelagh School

As I Listen And Wait

I can hear the bombs,
They're coming to kill me,
The zipping noise has stopped,
The bomb is falling.

My daddy is fighting,
My mummy is dead,
My sister is crying,
Tucked up in bed.

I am all alone,
There's no one to save me,
I will die a painful death,
But I guess that's how it's meant to be.

The bomb has fallen to the ground,
My heart is pounding within me,
A piece of brick hits my head,
I am left unconscious.

My side is being prodded,
I begin to sit up,
My sister sits there holding my hand,
Holding it tight.

I did not die a painful death,
I am alive for all to see,
My sister too is still by my side,
Just how it's meant to be.

Hannah Betts (13)
Ranelagh School

Troubles

From troubles of the world,
To troubles of my heart,
Even though we are together,
It's like we are apart.
I didn't mean to do this,
I didn't mean to stray,
So please listen
To what I have to say.
If only I could turn back time,
Undo the things I've done,
Unsay the things I said to you,
Go back to all our fun.
Now that I'm all alone,
I see what I have lost,
I see what I risked
And now I pay the cost.

Emma-Marie Pugh (14)
Ranelagh School

Falling

Hooked on a towering tree,
High above the sky,
A leaf flutters gracefully,
Now unattached it flies.

Drifting towards the ground,
Swept up by the morning breeze,
Dancing round, down and down,
Just one in a billion leaves.

Cushioned by the Earth's damp soil
As it moves along the christened grass,
Until resting in some plants, unspoiled,
Where its journey lasts!

Katherine Loudoun (13)
Ranelagh School

That'll Be The Day

The day when Mummy doesn't shout,
That'll be the day.
The day when I am not shut out,
That'll be the day.
The day when Daddy isn't cruel,
That'll be the day.
The day when I am liked at school,
That'll be the day.
The day when I can have fun,
That'll be the day.
The day when I can hug my mum,
That'll be the day.
The day when Daddy isn't tipsy,
That'll be the day.
The day when I'm not called a gypsy,
That'll be the day.
The day when Dad just stays at home,
That'll be the day.
The day when I don't feel alone,
That'll be the day.

Hayley Faulkner (13)
Ranelagh School

Rain In My Heart

It's raining in my heart today,
I've only sad feelings to show I've not much to say.

There are things that are upsetting me,
People ask me what's wrong, they won't let me be.

I don't want to tell them just how I feel,
About these feelings I have, I will not reveal.

What's troubling all my heart and soul,
The tears in my eyes I cannot control

Them from running and pouring down my cheeks.
These feelings have taken me over, I've admitted defeat.

Alice McGonnell (13)
Ranelagh School

Dreams Of Death

Death, dying,
Shooting, crying,
These are the sounds of war I can hear,
Loudly dripping in my sister's tear.

With leaders of cruelty fighting,
Bombs are hitting with flashes like lightning
Weapons of madness,
People of badness,
These are what I can see in my head,
Oh, I wish I was snug and safe in my bed.

Bang, bang! there goes the door,
There's someone coming I can hear them on the floor,
They've come in my room, I was prepared to be doomed.
As I open my eye,
I realise it is a lie.

Alex Boundy (12)
Ranelagh School

An Afternoon, Late Summer, In A Room

An afternoon, late summer, in a room,
a little flame flickers by a broom.
With the window open,
a small breeze fills the space.

An afternoon, late summer, in a room,
a bride sits waiting for her groom.
The door is ajar, with a hall beyond,
with only the world outside.

An afternoon, late summer, in a room,
a spider is about to face its doom.
A ladder going up, up, up
the darkness is a strange space.

An afternoon, late summer, in a room.

Ollie Martin (13)
Ranelagh School

Anything Poems

Water
Flowing, over the rocks and the sand
Shining, in the palm of God's hand
Dancing, in the light of the sun
Splashing, with our friends all as one.

Autumn
Colours of trees, leaves, clothes
Cold wind, chilling as it blows
Darker mornings, shorter days
God's wonderful world, seasons change.

Vision
See all around, God's creation, everything
Flowers, trees, animals, colours
Praise God for everything you can see
Eyes, sight, life, vision.

Killer whale
Huge, sea explorer, giant.
Consuming tiny fish, many
Rising up to the surface, magnificent
Lifting its tail, splash!

Snail
Slow, steady, slimy
Silver, squidgy, slidy
Small, sheltered, safe.
Slug, shell, snail.

Zoë Uffindell (12)
Ranelagh School

Foreign Lands

Up into a cherry tree,
Who should climb but little me?
I held the trunk with both my hands,
And looked abroad to foreign lands.

Winding up, winding down,
Through city, or through town.
Winding in, winding out,
Holding salmon, cod and trout.
Runs the Nile of Africa.

My gaze flicks to Iceland,
Where plenty of igloos stand.
This is where the snow bears sleep,
I like to watch them, as I peek.
How I wish to visit Iceland.

Deep, deep blue,
I really, really do,
Love the sea,
Just the fish and me.
Swimming in the ocean.

Green, green, green,
It makes me keen.
Down in the Amazon,
We run and hide,
While the animals glide.

In the distance there's sand,
Pyramids made by hand.
Let's raid the tombs,
Filled with many rooms
And hope to find treasure.

When I sleep I shall visit these places!

Annabelle Shearer (12)
Ranelagh School

How To Break Your Jaw

I gather my up speed,
I'm cycling as fast as I can go,
I think I can jump it indeed,
Or am I going too slow?

No I'm not!
I don't lift up my wheel,
I've definitely forgot,
Is this a dream or is it real?

I'm lying there on the floor,
Lying there in pain,
My fingers feel extremely sore,
To make that better from my jaw I start to feel a strain.

My friend lifts my bike off me,
I'm in a lot of shock,
It's a good thing I'd had my tea,
Because I'm off to see the doc!

From one hospital to another,
I can't speak at all,
It's a good thing someone rang my mother,
Suddenly I don't feel very cool.

My sister comes with me,
I'm relieved to see my mum,
My jaw doesn't look too good as far as the doc could see,
I keep getting shivers, my fingers are feeling numb,

I find out I've broken my jaw,
At hospital I stay overnight,
I get shown to my dark bedroom,
I can't sleep I'm in too much pain and fright.

Lauren Brown (12)
Ranelagh School

A Poem

Out I walk, with my friends,
Across the road, around the bend,
There before me lies the sea,
My friends and I, move forward with glee.

The water, it is very deep,
But so nice and warm that I could fall asleep,
Away I drift with the tide,
I hear the lifeguard shout,
'I'm okay,' I lie.

I sit up, where am I?
Have I drowned in the sea?
No, of course not, I'm alive,
And on a sunny beach,
I hope the inhabitants of this place aren't mutant freaks!

'Qu'est-ce que c'est?' says a man,
Staring down at me,
'Where am I?' I ask unhappily.
'You're in Calais,' the man replies.
'I've got to get back!' I cry.

I splash into the sea,
Look around, and count to three,
Then I swim as fast as I can,
Back to Dover and onto land.

I catch a ferry from the white cliffs
To take me to Appledore in a tick.

When I'm at home I tell my friends,
They don't believe me,
And . . .
That's the end!

Peter Fellows (12)
Ranelagh School

A Boy Called Harry!

Imagine a boy, eleven years old
Just a poor orphan, or so he'd been told . . .
But we find Harry Potter's no ordin'ry lad
An evil wizard murdered his mum and his dad.

So that's how we find him, parents are dead
And all Harry's got left is a scar on his head.
It's not until someone sends Harry a letter
From the wizarding world, that things start to get better.

So leaving behind a life that's been cruel
He starts his adventures at Hogwarts high school
He makes lots of friends and some enemies too
He discovers the truth about 'You know who'

Everyone watches him fly round the pitch
His favourite pastime, they call it Quidditch.
He's a natural Seeker, he glides through the air
If the Snitch is around he always knows where.

Excitement, adventure, the 'Philosopher's Stone'
He has dangers to face and he does it alone
He seeks his revenge, he couldn't be blamed
For his need to destroy 'he who shouldn't be named'

But don't let me ramble or reveal the full tale
As most of you know, the books are on sale.
So don't watch the TV, do your homework with speed
The story of Harry is an excellent read.

Kim Harrison (12)
Ranelagh School

Snow

Small, fluffy snowflakes fall from the grey skies
Icy and cold are the winds that blow
Stalactites hang from the end of my nose
Snow! Snow! Snow!

Body tingling from head to toe
Silhouette in the snow
Woollen gloves to keep hands warm
Hats and scarves pulled on tight
Big fur coats creamy white
Cold! Cold! Cold!

In the distant blue skies seen
A ray of sunshine begins to beam
As the snowman starts to melt
Our body temperature rises
A single ice crystal is left behind
Melt! Melt! Melt!

Danielle Adams (12)
Ranelagh School

Fireworks

One night of the year there's a noisy sound,
They are fireworks whizzing around,
Fireworks are noisy and they are quick,
They shoot up in the air with a click.

Fireworks are colourful and very bright,
People look up to see a beautiful sight,
Some stay up and some go *bang*
But some of them go *bang! Bang! Bang!*

People celebrate on Bonfire day,
With sparklers, for children to play,
Writing their names in the air,
A special day everywhere.

Benjamin Lam (13)
Ranelagh School

King Henry VIII

His face was twisted into a cruel smile
His little piggy eyes began to shine
His broad shoulders started to go up and down
As he laughed a thunderous laugh

His wrinkled white hand reached out and out
Towards the head that was
The head of a beautiful maiden of gold
Now an angel of Heaven

He picked up the pale and gloomy head
And stared at her big brown eyes
He then threw back the head
And looked down in disgust

He walked away with loping strides
And disappeared down the darkened corridor
Never to see the head again
And so it is buried in the deserted graveyard.

Joseph Cole (12)
Ranelagh School

The Fish

The fish swims slowly through the water
Glimmering in the sun
Shimmering all its beautiful, brilliant colours
It checks its path, as sensing danger in the water
Then from the murky blue, the danger ever closer
The predator sneaking up on its prey
The shark creeps up behind the fish ever waiting
Then like a Jack-in-the-box springs the attack
The fish, agile as ever, darts between rocks
The shark ever nearing
Then the crack that would give the fish an escape route
Only metres away, it makes a final dash and gets away.

Sam Clothier (13)
Ranelagh School

Free Spirit

Her arms stretch skyward,
Her hair whipped the beach,
She threw up the ships,
Just out of reach.

She beat at the cliffs,
With tightly clenched hands,
She swept round the harbour,
And onto the sands.

She blew up the clouds,
She hurled down the rain,
She streamed up the beach,
And back down again.

She leapt up high,
She dived down low,
She threw up the torrents,
She blew up the flow.

She put out the flame,
From the watchman's lamp;
With the wind and the rain,
And the cold and the damp.

She calmed down with grief,
For the people passed,
And looked sparkling blue
And as clear as glass.

Alice Pocock (12)
Ranelagh School

As I Look Out Of My Window

As I look out of my window,
I see a view of green.
Bushes, trees and plants
And flowers that had not before been seen.

The birds are drinking from the pond,
And eating worms from the ground,
The insects are buzzing
And are busily flying around.

The trees sway in the wind,
The grass all green and lush,
There is movement on the garden floor
And upon it stands a mistle thrush.

Flowers are bright and plentiful,
Daffodils and English rose,
Orange, pink, blue,
They all stand in an upright pose.

Out of my window,
All of this I can see.
How wonderful nature can be!

Emma Wallace (12)
Ranelagh School

The Rose

A rose so beautiful,
Means so much,
With petals so intricate
And thorns that draw blood,
But the flower alone,
Symbolises love.

Luke Miller (13)
Ranelagh School

The Garden Flower Haiku

The garden flower
Is a very small seedling
And slowly it grows.

The garden flower
Is slowly getting taller
And taller again.

The garden flower
Is slowly starting to bloom
The petals have come.

The garden flower
Is looking so beautiful
Tall and elegant.

The garden flower
Has been here for a long while
So slowly it dies.

The garden flower
Has withered and perished now
The flower is dead.

Samantha Burgisser (12)
Ranelagh School

Autumn

Autumn, autumn,
I love autumn,
Leaves are falling from the trees.

Red, yellow, brown,
Floors of colour,
Picking conkers on our knees.

Timothy Rye (12)
Ranelagh School

France

France, who needs it?
What's in it?
The Eiffel Tower - so what!
I have a model of it in my room,
You trudge up all those steps,
Listening to an over-happy tour guide,
Practically singing,
'You're almost there
Only 265 thousand steps to go!'
And then when you do reach the top,
All you see are fields on one side,
And solid concrete on the other!
And after using up all your energy,
All you can eat are snails and frogs' legs!
But even if you did want something to eat,
You can't order it,
Because the waiter can't understand you,
So all you can order are fromage frais!

Je déteste le Français.

Rosie Hill (12)
Ranelagh School

Secret Forest

At night, by fire
Hunters roam the skies
Paths lit by nocturnal lights
As the sound of silence echoes.
Geldings shuffle to and fro,
As campers sleep in shadows.
The motionless lake sits in sorrow
While wolves hunt round its shallows,
Up in the trees an eagle sounds
Hunting for its prey,
The moon's glow surrounds the forest
As a hundred tales are told.

Amy Peacock (14)
Ranelagh School

Remember Me

Remember me when I'm gone away
Lying in a dark, cold coffin
Still and quiet here I lay
Now there's no more time to play

My life used to be so full of fun
I thought it would never end
I hate the dark, I miss the sun
This is what I have become

Am I still loved and missed?
When was the last time that we kissed?
Is your heart still torn and broken
When you knew I couldn't be woken?

So here I am still lying here
Never forget I love you dear
I think about you day and night
I look at you and see the light.

Stephen Newey (13)
Ranelagh School

I Have Never Been In Your Position

I have never been in your position
I don't know how you feel
I would be very upset
I'd think that I'd got an unfair deal

I have never been in your position
I don't know what to say
I can't say, grin and bear it
I can't say, smile, it's OK.

I have never been in your position
I don't know what you see
I'd like to see someone there
And for you that someone is me.

Jasmin Shearer (14)
Ranelagh School

Singing

Singing is my life,
Singing is my soul,
When I sing I feel a joy,
It really makes me whole.

Singing is a pleasure,
Singing for me is fun,
I could never get enough,
It never makes me numb.

I'm singing through the days,
I'm singing through the nights,
When it gets to morning light,
Cats all start to fight.

Now I'm getting annoyed,
A little frustrated too,
My teacher plays a 'la' note,
I surprisingly shout out a 'boo'.

The stupid neighbours are growling now,
I'm wondering what to do,
Shut up right now I'm singing a song,
They shout out, 'Amazing! What new?'

Zara Mirza (13)
Ranelagh School

At Night By The Fire

At night by the fire the fairies dance,
Sing, twirl, smile and prance,
Their dresses are made out of silk and satin,
They all have their own individual pattern.

Their hair is blonde ringlets and curls,
Their necklaces are made out of big, expensive pearls,
At night by the fire the fairies dance,
Sing, twirl, smile and prance.

Claudia Duncan (13)
Ranelagh School

Raining In My Heart

Looking back on how we used to be
How you were, always there for me
But now you're gone
Everything seems wrong
Since we've been apart
I can't stop this raining in my heart

This rain won't stop falling
I'm so unhappy you're not calling
What can I do to change your mind?
All these memories I can't leave behind
Since we've been apart
I can't stop this raining in my heart

Always thought you'd be with me only
But now it's killing me slowly
Every time I see your face
It seems I am in a different place
Since we've been apart
I can't stop this raining in my heart

I wish you were here with me now
But you're not and I know that somehow
I must find a way to get over you
And find someone new
Now we are apart
I must stop this raining in my heart.

Amy Gray (13)
Ranelagh School

Remember Me

Remember me when I'm gone away
I may never see you again.
I hope to see you another day
Do not miss me and write to me with your pen.

Remember me when I'm gone away
As the seasons change and the leaves fall down.
We will once again be joyous and gay
As the summer comes the sun wears its crown.

Remember me when I'm gone
Will you miss me? I wonder.
Remember me in some other way
Maybe as you slumber.

Remember me when I'm gone away
How will you fill your time?
What will you do with your time?
But remember me when you see my sign.

Matthew Higginson (13)
Ranelagh School

The Horrors Of War

The artillery fire over your head.
The officer shouts the order to fire;
You wish you were at home in bed,
But instead you open fire.

You see a soldier in your sights,
You pull the trigger - *click, click*.
The gun is empty, you reload,
You open the pack - *flick, flick*.

You load the gun and aim,
The officer yells a command.
You decide whether to kill or maim,
You decide to kill and fire.

Matthew Clitherow (13)
Ranelagh School

Clovelly

Set in the countryside of Devon -
Famous for its rocky hills . . .
Famous for the super stonework . . .
Famous for its paths.
The paths are like mountains.
There it is,
With its absurdly unbelievable views,
There it is: it's Clovelly.

Peaceful setting as we climb those steps.
I must be careful not to slip
On one side there's the scrumptious seashore
On the other there are the views
On either side gift shops galore.

The gift shops are full of different chewy fudges
Chocolate, vanilla and lots more of other fantastic flavours
There are the clotted cream cakes, biscuits
But nothing beats the scrumptious-looking scones
With fun-packed fillings
Jam, butter, clotted creams
That tease the tastebuds badly.

Abbey Short (13)
Ranelagh School

Autumn

One whole year turning into oranges and reds once again,
Ploughing through the leaves, playing with my friends.
A warming spectrum of glistening gold
Tinting the oak trees, withered and old.

Animals prepare for the frosty winter ahead;
Birds line up like soldiers at inspection for flight.
Squirrels harvesting food ready for hibernation
And smuggle it back to their secret location.

Rachel Dyer (12)
Ranelagh School

River's Surprise

He is sound in his home,
Deep in a valley,
Preparing for an evening walk.

He has green-blue eyes,
His skin is brown.

River starts to run swiftly,
Silently, calmly.

His voice is quiet at times when he is happy,
But when he is angry it is loud.
River is restless and speedy.

He ends his journey in London where a crowd is waiting
He turns and goes home.

Jon Cope (13)
Ranelagh School

Concorde

This supersonic jet
Cruises across the Atlantic
At twice the speed of sound!

Air France created this bird,
Although you may not have heard,
They are taking her out of service!

Concorde flew from the USA to France and UK,
But sadly that is coming to an end,
With so many tragic accidents
They are bringing it to a close.

It has become too costly to run,
With no one to take on board.
The only other trip it'll take is to the nearest museum,
Argh, what an end to such an era.

Matthew Wyles (12)
St Bernard's Convent School, Slough

Watching The Sky

See how it dances, see how it twirls,
Stars scattered about like a string of pearls,
The bleakness of blackness, the moon's white arc,
The silence and quiet that belongs to the dark.

And now it is light, white clouds against blue,
And the whiteness breaks and the sun shines through,
And through the clouds, the sun must endure,
'Til the clouds disappear and the sunlight is pure.

And even then, the great blue can stray,
It can take on a form of dull, stone-grey,
And the sun does not shine and the rain falls like tears,
All through the day 'til the moon reappears.

So the sun sinks and dark reigns over light,
With just the moon, a tiny circle, yet shining so bright,
From dark back to light, from day back to night,
So sit waiting, watching, the sky and all her delights.

Natalie D'Lima (12)
St Bernard's Convent School, Slough

Winter

Winter came and autumn vanished,
No more sunshine, no more warmth.
Winter engulfing the towns with snow,
Leaving icicles as he goes.

The cold wind nipping ferociously,
And the snow stifling the ground.
Snowflakes twirling and swirling in the bitter air,
And covering the trees in a soft white blanket.

The wind worsened
And turned into a blizzard.
Winter carries on, never to die,
Until the sun plucks up courage to shine!

Hannah Shearer (11)
St Bernard's Convent School, Slough

Rugby

He fearlessly stepped onto the wind-blown pitch,
The crowd emitting a deafening roar,
He was feeling anxious but still remaining focused,
Feeling proud to wear the shirt that he wore,

The referee placed the whistle unto his lips,
Blowing with gusto to commence the game,
The kicker placing the ball high in the air,
Exactly reaching his aim.

The players dashed with urgent haste
To the spot where the ball would land,
The ball was expertly caught with perfect timing,
As another cheer rose up from the stand.

The two sides battled on,
The importance to score was paramount,
But a flawless pass and a faultless kick,
Opened the scoring account.

In the course of the first half the sides were close,
Until the referee's whistle did chime,
The players trudged off the field,
It was the beginning of half-time.

Quite soon after that the players were back out,
The players eager to start the game, the crowd eager to see,
The match was soon underway once more,
But which side would clinch the vital victory?

The referee inspected,
The players' performance sublime,
The match had come to its end,
The whistle blown for the final time.

One team and their fans went home sad,
One team and their fans went home contented,
But the winners weren't on the trip home too soon,
Because the trophy had to be presented.

Jack Tompkins (13)
St Bernard's Convent School, Slough

Caught In The Middle

The wind is high,
The sea is low,
But I'm caught in the middle.

The bird is left,
The boat is right,
But I'm caught in the middle!

I'm stuck in the middle,
What should I do?
Should I play in the fields
Or just wait in the middle?

Until that day when I become the end,
Should I write a poem about the end?
But I think now,
As I look back 40 years ago,
All this time I have been content
Being caught in the middle!

Katharine Hurden (12)
St Bernard's Convent School, Slough

Wizard's Words

Hubble bubble trolls and trouble
Dying burns and cauldron bubble

Fire name and fire make
In the water we must take
Eye of newt and tail of cat
Leg of pig and wing of bat
Teeth of snake and tongue of frog
Blind worm head and paw of dog
For some harm and powerful trouble
Burn a boil and get some bubbles

Hubble bubble trolls and trouble
Dying burns and cauldron bubble.

Marcus Connolly (12)
St Bernard's Convent School, Slough

What?

I like to talk to purple trees
And play with lions in the sea.

There is a place you do not know,
With summer islands full of snow.

I cannot see who you are,
You look distinct from afar.

But then again, the autumn leaves,
Illuminate your invisible sleeves.

Who am I? You want to know,
From a place I cannot grow.

What is more, I really am,
Non-existent of all land.

Joseph Rohde (11)
St Bernard's Convent School, Slough

At The Door . . .

There came a knocking at the door,
I opened it and there I saw,
A man all dressed in black and red,
A large black cap upon his head.

It was him. At once I knew,
I thought very quickly, *what should I do?*
I flew upstairs, locked the door,
Hid under the bed on the dusty floor.

That didn't work, he had many ways,
Escaping him was like a maze.
He sniffed me out, held the knife,
I knew this was the end of my life . . .

Zara Livingston (12)
St Bernard's Convent School, Slough

My Perfect Friend

I want a friend to stick up for me
To lock up a secret and throw away the key.
I want a friend to be loving and sharing
For when I am hurt she will be caring.

I want a friend who I can talk to and tell her all my worries
I want my friend to forgive me, when I am wrong and I am sorry.
I want my friend to sometimes have a laugh, but can be serious as well
I want a friend who I can trust and who I can tell secrets and not tell.

I want a friend who I can joke about with and also who can be truthful
I want a friend who invites me round for tea and is always faithful.
I want a friend I can play with and has similar interests to me
I want a friend not to laugh at me, not to be bossy so I can feel free!

Do you know the right friend for me?

Georgina Hambi (12)
St Bernard's Convent School, Slough

Inside A Computer

Inside the computer the little men thrive,
running to and fro, trying to hide.
But every now and then, you'll catch a glimpse of them,
as they run across your screen.
Inside a computer, these little men run back and forth,
fetching documents and pictures, faster than before,
then, when the computer is turned off, they rest again.
In this world of wires, when a little man tires,
he is given a break and another springs awake.
In this world of little men an army also thrives,
protecting your computer and all the little men's lives.
Inside a computer . . .
Shut down.

Daniel Cassidy (12)
St Bernard's Convent School, Slough

Synaesthesia Moods

(Synaesthesia: Synaesthesia is a rare condition. Nobody has the same type.
It means that you can taste sounds, and days of the week are colours,
but it differs from person to person)

Your lips are a slug, wet and slimy,
they twist up into a mocking smile.
They open into a cave, dark and damp.
Bitter, sharp lemons shoot out of the cave,
                              flying bullets.

Your hair is swamp and seaweed
grasping waves, on a stormy sea.
You turn your head and flick your storm,
icy nails and bloody daggers slice the air,
                              stinging faces.

Your skin is warm caramel, whispering to me,
you look at me and I stare,
a deep aqua ocean in your eyes.
As I watch, dolphins and fish leap out,
                              into the sky.

I taste candyfloss and buttered pancakes,
your hair is woven of golden honey.
It dances through the air, twisting around.
I catch my breath, but you are still there,
                    a figure of my imagination.

Iona McKendrick (12)
St Bernard's Convent School, Slough

The Shadow

As my head slips under the covers,
I feel a chill down my spine.
I know it is the time of the evening when it visits me.

The crepiffling beast comes slithding in my room,
It looks around and stares at me,
Then it laughs an evirifying laugh.

It skinces on my walls,
It frightens me so much,
As the cripstery monster comes forward to try and grab me.

Now by this point I am trembling,
The monster has never gone this far,
I shudder to think what it might do to me next.

Then oh my wonbouifoine hero comes to rescue me,
All is light now and the villain has disappeared,
Hooray, hooray what a beautvely night.

Crepiffling: creepy, shuffling and terrifying.
Slithding: riding and slithering.
Evirifying: evil and horrifying.
Skinces: dances and skips.
Cripstery: crippling, scary and monstrous.
Wonbouifoine: heroine, fabulous, terrific and wonderful.
Beautvely: lovely and beautiful.

Melissa Hickey (11)
St Bernard's Convent School, Slough

Where Was He?

He knelt there, waiting
His hand on his lover's head
The far-off cry of long-lost love
Had forsaken this forlorn bed

Where was God in this time of suffering?
Where was He when thousands died?
Where is He when a good man is dying?
His love by his side

Perhaps God did not approve
Of this union of two men
Had He left them waiting
For their journeys both to end?

The lover kneeling there, waiting
Let out an animal cry
Again he heard those whispered words
Both live or both they die

He knelt there praying to God
'Spare him, take me,' he cried
Maybe God ignored his prayer
Because that good man died.

Madelaine Wood (12)
St Bernard's Convent School, Slough

The Witch

Riding on a *slold* broomstick,
And *cacklaugs* as she goes,
At dead of night
The devil,
The *massugly*,
It is . . .
The witch!

Alongside her a
Moofy creature
With *scamass*, bulging, bright yellow eyes.
Licking its brown *grubgly* paws.
Riding on through the night,
This *gloosome animal*
With warts on her head and nose
Wolides the night skies
Cauldron, spells and wicked yells
Are to be seen and heard at
Hallowe'en.
Who is it?

The devil,
The *massugly*
It is . . .
The witch!

Máireád Greene (11)
St Bernard's Convent School, Slough

Impact

You would never expect it,
Just like me,
But it came, oh yes it did.
The thought, even the consideration,
Just sends me back.

There's me just a lone rider,
A lucky kid I was.
To survive the initial blast,
Was a miracle in itself.

The pillbox was my holy ground,
My eternal gratefulness.
My life was spared,
From the unforgiving blast
That was to be the demise of millions.

Then came the thirst,
The very thing that sent me willingly to my deathbed.
But my saddlebag provided me with a chocolate bar
And so my unyielding journey went on.

The little energy that chocolate gave me,
Led me on, on into the unbelievable truth.

Joseph Johnston (13)
St Bernard's Convent School, Slough

The Deep Blue Sea

Have you ever heard of the deep blue sea?
It lays in wait for you and me,
It's like a monster, a great big massolent monster!

The sea attacks the beach with a terrimongous tide,
It wants you to run, it wants you to hide.
With the *ginormity* of its power,
It will make you feel quakified!

It is like a door, a door of opportunities to prove your worth.
The quantity of these doors comes in squinbillions!

'I want to learn more of this deep blue sea,
Does it really lie in wait for you and me?'

'Is it really deepilicious?'
'Is it really blue?'
Stop asking me questions and I will tell you.

I heard the deep blue sea talk the other day,
It said, 'Sssswwwiiissshhh . . . ssswwwooossshhh . . .

Splash!'

Then it asked me if I had ever heard
Of the deep blue sea?

I said, 'No can you please tell me?'

Huw Rosen (11)
St Bernard's Convent School, Slough

My Poem

My dog is biglar, haifluff and smelly
It always annoys me when he blocks the telly.

His nose is cowet
Like a fish caught in a net.

He has round, moiswe brown eyes
But they're hardly open from sunset to sunrise.

He doesn't frolay, his life is a bore
It sounds like thunning when he snores.

He never goes out to frolay in the sun
'He's a useless lump,' says everyone.

But I don't care what they say, I love my dog
And that's the way it will stay.

Biglar = big and large
Haifluff = hairy and fluffy
Cowet = cold and wet
Moiswe = moist and wet
Frolay = frolic and play
Thunning = thunder and lightning.

Sarah Cook (11)
St Bernard's Convent School, Slough

I Hate Writing Poems

Writing a poem,
May seem quite a simple thing to do.
But putting your thoughts and feelings down on paper,
Can get you in a stew.

Deciding on what adjectives to use,
May sound quite easy.
But when you start to put them down,
They can sound quite cheesy.

I never seem to have ideas,
My brain just goes dead.
I sit there with a blank piece of paper
And an empty head.

I hate writing poems,
And they are some of my reasons why.
So if a teacher asks me to write one,
I really wanna cry.

Danielle Donoghue (12)
St Bernard's Convent School, Slough

What Am I?

I'm sometimes warm, sometimes cold
Sunsets turn me from blue to gold.
Winter's cold, that's what I hate,
But summer's fun, it's worth the wait.

When I'm angry, I get rough,
Don't get close, I'll be mad enough.
But you can come and see me
On summer's days - I'm full of glee!

If you're down or feeling blue,
Come to see me, I'll comfort you.
There's only six more of me . . .
So, what am I? I am the sea.

Rose Maini (12)
St Bernard's Convent School, Slough

The Crocodile

As I went walking, one morn',
I met a crocodile, with one eye torn.
I asked the crocodile, 'What happened to you?
What made you go One Eye Hue?'

'You don't want to know what happened,'
The crocodile replied.
'Just in case I told you the wrong story and lied
You see, I have no short term memory,
It is so bad, so terribly!'
A crocodile with no memory is so mad!
As mad as my balding dad!

'Wait a minute,' as I paused for thought,
Thinking about what I had been taught.
'Wait a minute, crocodiles don't talk,
As jellyfish don't walk.'
(Another minute) 'I know, I heard you speak!'
But the crocodile's mouth did not open a tweak.

Daniel Vidal (12)
St Bernard's Convent School, Slough

Hallowe'en

Once a year the witches fly
On their broomsticks through the sky,
A black cat stares into space
Whilst the children carve a pumpkin's face!

Children dress up and go out at night
And give some old ladies quite a fright,
The children think they've seen a ghost
But really it's only the party host.

The skeletons rattle in the homes
Whilst the ghosts let out some loud groans
Everyone's excited because they want to go out
Then they all shout
Trick or treat!

Charlotte Stevens (12)
St Bernard's Convent School, Slough

The Last Soldier Left

When I look into the fields of Sundy,
There's nothing there to see,
Nothing but the quarry of bones buried under me,
For no one pays any respect anymore,
No young, no old
No one speaks of the battle because no one is told,
No one talks of the soldiers who fought to their best,
Because there were no other men
No other men that were left.

When I look into the fields of Sundy,
There's no one here to cry,
No one to cry in the day or under the night sky.
I saw the soldier fight
I saw the soldiers die
I saw the bloodstained grass beneath the starry sky.
No one talks of the soldiers who fought to their best,
Because there were no other men
No other men that were left.

When I look into the fields of Sundy
One thing I cannot see -
Why did fate take them
Instead of taking me?

Why was I the one left? I can't take it anymore!
The burden that I carry has become very sore!
No one talks of the soldiers who fought to their best,
Because I was the soldier,
The soldier that was left.

Tom Mckeown (12)
St Bernard's Convent School, Slough

To A Hurricane Pilot Of 504 Squadron - 15th September 1940

Did the sun wake you early that morning
When the Luftwaffe were coming to call?
Were you clumsy when you dressed to be ready?
Did you kiss goodbye the photo on your wall?

Did your ground crew try hard to be cheerful
As they checked every buckle and strap?
Did they take extra care with your engine?
Did you study more closely your map?

When the order came to scramble, were you fearful?
Could you breathe as you soared in the air?
When you spotted the enemy coming
Did you go into fight with hope and a prayer?

Were those seconds of battle terrifying
As you soared towards the bombers to attack?
Was there pressure in your chest, could you think clearly,
With bursting bullets and screaming planes at your back?

When the flames ripped off your wing, did you panic?
Did you fight to control your stricken plane?
I saw you spiral down to Earth, your chute billowing,

And, I thank God for your courage - again.

Tom Bausor (12)
St Bernard's Convent School, Slough

Joe And Jon And John-Joe And The Purple Toad

Joe and Jon and John-Joe
One day walked along the road,
When suddenly in front of them
Fell a big, fat, purple toad!

All three of them, both shocked and scared,
Leapt back with sheer surprise,
For they could not believe what was
Before their very eyes.

The toad stood there and stared at them
It sensed their disbelief,
It said, 'Please now, I mean no harm,
I do not mean to cause such grief.'

And at these words, the threesome ceased
Their panicky behaviours,
The toad continued, 'Do not panic!
For I'm a magical toad, young sirs!'

Joe, Jon and John-Joe looked in awe
While the toad opened its mouth once more,
'Now I'd like to think you'd like one wish.'
(When it said this, these men dropped their jaw.)

'But for this to happen, you must first
Hand me your wallets, one by one,
Then, afterwards, I'll grant you your wish
And hopefully business will be done.'

So the foolish men gave the toad their wallets
Not knowing what it had in mind,
The toad then leapt off without saying goodbye
The whole wishing scheme had just been a lie!

Next time you see one on the road
Never trust a purple toad!

Elwin Carlos (12)
St Bernard's Convent School, Slough

The Creature

Up on the top of an icy mountain,
Lives a creature so evil that Hell spat it back out,
It has blood-red eyes and teeth like knives,
And human flesh is on what it survives.

Its fur is pitch-black and its hair standing on end,
Go near it and you'll come to a messy end,
Many have tried to defeat in vain,
Their skulls lie like trophies in the creature's resting place.

My father tried to defeat it,
He took his vorpal sword in hand,
He raised it up, didn't stand a chance,
The creature killed him and tore him apart,
How many more will this dreaded thing cost?

The townsfolk are planning to kill the evil thing,
They are organising an army to shun it away,
I will join them and may die on this day,
We will leave at midnight carrying torches and pitchforks,
And ambush the horror wherever it lurks.

'There is the cave,' someone did shout,
And we ran in cursing it to hell,
But curses were not enough and like flies many fell,
Not many were left but onwards we fought,
I was determined to kill it, and avenge my father's death,
So I hurled my pitchfork into the air,
I waited and watched as my deadly weapon struck,
It plunged into the creature down into its back,
It let off a blood-curdling scream and that was that.

The people live happy now; they have nothing to fear,
And I'm sure my father rests easy,
The creature is no longer near.

Jack Makepeace (12)
St Bernard's Convent School, Slough

Candlelight

I sit alone in that dark corner
A small flick of a candle
A howl of a wolf
And a whisper of the wind
Is all I can see and hear

I can no longer move, I'm paralysed
I'm just sitting and staring
At the small candle flame
In my dark corner
No one else but me

I start to wonder about life
It is too short
What is it really about?
Does anyone really care?
Life is like the flick of my candle.

I see a rat and it sees me
It scuttles past and ignores me
Just like the rest of the world
I'm an outsider
Now, I only have my candle.

Nastasia Bishop (12)
St Bernard's Convent School, Slough

The Weather

Speeding 'cross the ground
The wind and the cloud
Making whistling sounds
Echoing quiet and loud

High up in the air
Bright up in the sky
The shining sun up there
In the blue, up high

Old and dark and grey
Raining down and down
A dark and gloomy day
A pitter-patter sound

A hail of glistening white
Of frost, of flake, of snow
The sky with snow alight
A cold yet warming glow

A hail of glistening white
Old and dark and grey
High up in the air
Speeding 'cross the ground.

Jamie William Abbott (12)
St Bernard's Convent School, Slough

The Cruise

Tickets for a cruise!
Tickets for a cruise!
All the way to the Med,
Climb aboard!
Climb aboard!
You will even be fed.

Hurry up!
Hurry up!
Don't wait too long,
Buy now!
Buy now!
For soon they'll all be gone.

Come on in!
Come on in!
The luxury you will see,
Here's your room!
Here's your room!
The most comfortable you'll ever be.

Settle down!
Settle down!
For soon we'll be on our way,
Here we go!
Here we go!
We'll be there within a day.

We're almost there!
We're almost there!
Have you enjoyed your stay?
Here we are!
Here we are!
Come aboard another day.

Morag White (12)
St Bernard's Convent School, Slough

My New Toy

When will the day end?
When will it be Monday?
I've never ever felt this way
About a day that isn't Sunday

I've this new toy you see
And I wanna show the class
One more day to go you see
And I'll be running on the grass

With my new toy in one hand
And the old in the other
I'll be as happy as a lamb
Dancing with its mother

My Pokémon cards are in the bin
My marbles are under the bed
My teddies are in the cupboard today
I've got a new toy instead

I went to school Monday morning
I couldn't wait for today
I walked into class and sat at my desk
All the kids shout out and say,

'That toy's yesterday's news, ha ha!'
And, 'What rubbish things!'
I slumped down in my chair
It hurt inside and stings

Oh well I think to myself,
I wonder what toy I'll get next
I want a mobile phone, wicked!
And then I'll be able to text.

Freddie Heffernan (12)
St Bernard's Convent School, Slough

The Seasons

The joy of spring comes and goes,
All that winter loves and loathes.
The leaves and flowers blossom all around,
They grow and open without a sound.

Laughing children in the park,
Hours and hours until dark.
The bright colours of summer are everywhere,
Then autumn comes and all is bare.

All the leaves of the old oak tree,
Have all gone like the birds and bees.
All that was warm is now bleak,
And the chills of winter return within a week.

The snowflakes fall so delicately,
They form on the ground, a snow-like sea.
The winter's frost and coldness still here,
The arrival of spring will soon be near.

Sean Morgan (12)
St Bernard's Convent School, Slough

Boys And Girls

I really don't understand girls
You think I understand boys.
Always playing with Barbie dolls
Always fighting with Action Man toys.
Why do they wear so much make-up?
Why do they gel back their hair?
Why do they have such high heels?
They think girls really care!
Girls just wanna look good
Boys just wanna be cool
Girls, I must say, are really quite weird
And boys are just big fools!

Emma Biasiolo (12)
St Bernard's Convent School, Slough

The Hidden Garden

The hidden garden lies
Tucked away from our sight,
Sleeping so peacefully
All through the night

The morning comes,
The sun awakes,
The birds are singing
As dawn breaks

The leaves are rustling,
As a light breeze blows,
The trees are swaying
And a small stream flows

The splashing of the water
Trickling down the stream
Awakes the hidden garden
From its hidden dream

The bees buzz round from flower to flower,
The birds soar up to the clear, blue sky,
The butterflies flit and dance about
While the time goes rushing by

The sun has set
And darkness falls
All is quiet
Within its walls

The hidden garden lies
Tucked away from our sight,
Sleeping so peacefully
All through the night.

Sarah Spriggs (12)
St Bernard's Convent School, Slough

Changing

Treacherous icy roads upon a winter's walk,
Upon a winter walk.
Icy cold,
Frosty as he talks.

Frosted windows glittering,
Icicles sparkling high.
Twinkling and flickering,
Up in the sky.

Ice outlines leaves,
Can you feel the breeze?
Leaves upon the ground,
Skeletons of trees.

Cold and shivery
The moonlight bare.
Snowflakes falling,
You could sit there and stare.

When you wake up the very next day,
From your bed where you lay.
You will see what's happened through a winter's night,
Changing through forecast, changing through sight.

Icicles sparkle in the bare moonlight,
Shimmering and glimmering, what a sight.
You want to see it all again,
But you have no choice and he melts at last.

Lisa Boweren (13)
St Bernard's Convent School, Slough

You're Not There

I say, 'Hello,' but you're not there
All I can do is stand and stare
I shout your name, but there is no answer
So still, I stand there by that room

That room that I cannot enter, it fills my heart with pain
Your voice still echoes in my mind
But you're gone now, and it doesn't make sense
May my meeting again with you be soon?

Your picture is on my wall and is fading fast
The one where you were helping others in the past
Patiently collecting, supporting the cause
Giving life to people who had been in distress.

I will go to your grave again and again
And pray for you, whose heart was full of gold
And then may we be together again at last
Because the pain is great now you're not here.

Justine Wilson (12)
St Bernard's Convent School, Slough

The Stream

It flows along like a dream,
The water trickling down the stream.
It shimmers in the sun's light,
Sparkling nicely, looking bright.

The birds sing, high and low,
But this can't distract me from the stream's glow.
I see fish swimming around,
Innocently, not making a sound.

All that I hear is the distant sound of a barking hound,
A fisherman singing, a distant ringing.
But all that I care about is in my sight,
The gleaming stream, twinkling bright.

Anna Townsend (12)
St Bernard's Convent School, Slough

There Is No Such Thing As Humans

I have a ghost that lives in my room
And do you know what it just said
It said, 'Mum I'm scared of the dark you know
So I'm going to bury my head

I'm sure I heard a scary noise
Mummy where's my cuddly ted?
I've been searching for him for ages
I just want to get to bed

And, again another horrible sound
It sounded like a roar,
Something is coming up the stairs
Now it's near the bedroom door.'

'I don't want any that nonsense now,'
Said Mummy ghost. 'Not a peep
There is no such thing as humans
Now try and get some sleep.'

Tom Sturt (12)
St Bernard's Convent School, Slough

The World In A True Light

In this world of war and death,
Why do people love and cherish it?
A man strangles a girl,
A person dies,
A family cries,
A car crash, a person will never walk again
The list goes on and on.
Yet still through the ashes of war, death and disabilities,
A smile will come,
A person will love again and the world will go on
The world is not perfect
But cherish it because one day you will lose it.

Claire Gill (11)
St Bernard's Convent School, Slough

The London Match

I can remember, the 9th of September
The London derby match.

The crowd were aligning so eager to catch
The London derby match.

They said in the paper that the 'odds were against them',
But we're gonna prove them wrong.
Cos
We won't be joking 'bout going home soaking
In glory, joy and victory.

The rivals they're scared,
For they have dared,
To watch the match with us.
Cos
Shouting, singing, cursing and
Winning
Is all we think and do!

Golden boy is on the ball, the crowd are off their seats,
He skips past one and again and again
And fires a wondrous shot.
It shatters the net but on the wrong side
Oh how did he put it wide?

The whistle is blown, the match has ended,
The ref is in relief.
He's off already before the players,
He knows we'll cause mischief.
I didn't want a draw, I wanted something more,
But there's nothing that I can do.

But that was last year and this is now
And we're at home this week.

Nick Carey (12)
St Bernard's Convent School, Slough

'Twas Cold Today

If this is to be my future, my all, everything that is to become of me
Then may the good grace of God, save His strength
For a waste it is to use it on me.

They say what I did was heresy
Blasphemy, wicked and wrong
Yet I remain quite unashamed
Like an unsure child
Unaware that the curse he has just uttered,
Straight from the lips of his father
Has silenced the room of petty ones . . .
Who are really just children themselves.

So as I bend over and the frost bites at my lips
I kneel and I hear a woman cry out in agony
A soft moan escapes my lips
For it is as if it were Christ Himself, shouting.

Shouting for the life of His child . . .
The Black Devil is coming.
I can hear footsteps ringing out across the silent courtyard,
The show is about to begin.

It's almost as if through some divine inspiration
I know what to do.

A slow smile spreads across my face.
I am at peace, oh so nearly there,
And suddenly nothing can touch me, nothing matters
For it's all insignificant now,
I am in my own sphere of joy . . . so nearly.

The demon rears, clutching at its blade
Fangs a-tremble.
And at last -
The cold lethargy that has waited so long
Seeps out of my bones.
I am home.

Lorna Berry (12)
St Bernard's Convent School, Slough

Wasted Through Hatred

Embedded into the fragments of time is a hatred,
A hatred that is not obvious,
But is created through jealousy, cowardice and distrust,
And which is subtle but lethal;
A hatred that speaks through a language of no words,
And an agonising violence that injures through no contact.

A magnolia with the destiny to flourish in a wasteland,
And with the capability to grow and bloom,
To live, to inspire, to display its radiance to the world,
Is suffocated and strangled by the bitter resentment
of the smaller weeds.
These are the original inhabitants, the beings intent on
devouring all goodness.
To deny the flower its very life-blood and chance to thrive.

As it cries out in silent sorrow,
Its brilliance and beaming colour slowly disappears
into the abyss,
And with the little strength that remains within,
It prepares to face the now enormous weeds and the
callous world beyond,
Although feeble, timid and desperate,
The once inferior beings have now conquered its soul
And are gradually weakening it in their jealous, sadistic wrath.

As the grey squirrel overwhelms the habitat of the red,
So we must think of the impact that we make upon each other,
As whilst we damage the minds of our fellows,
As we discriminate against those who are different,
And as we abuse the rights of others.
We are actually destroying the diversity of the world
that we live in,
A diversity that so enriches our lives.

David-Jason Gordon (12)
St Bernard's Convent School, Slough

Buffy

It came today
So small and so fluffy
It's black and grey
Its name is Buffy

It's six weeks old
And very sweet
It's as precious as gold
And likes to eat

It chews a red slipper
Morning and night
It's a little nipper
Lovely and light

It loves its walks
It's so energetic
But it hardly talks
And loves to lick

It sometimes has accidents
When it misses the mat
It chews the fence
And chases my cat

I love my new puppy
I couldn't live without it
It's really quite nutty
And never wants to sit

Holly Brennan (12)
St Bernard's Convent School, Slough

Moving House

I think we're moving house quite soon,
But I'm not sure quite when.
Maybe in a few months time
Or maybe next weekend.

Packing into boxes,
Clearing out my desk.
'Look! a piece of jigsaw,
Oh look, and here's the rest!'

Sorting out the cupboard,
Sorting out the shed.
'I lost this marble years ago!
What's this? It's old Ted!'

Packing everything away,
My teddies, toys and books.
Take down all my posters
And that dressing gown hook.

Clearing out the garage
And my old toy chest.
'You don't need that anymore!'
'But it's better than the rest!'

Taping up the boxes
I need to stop and think,
There must be something wrong here,
Cos here's the kitchen sink!

I think we're moving house quite soon,
But I'm not sure quite when!
Maybe before the next full moon
Or when I'm one hundred and ten!

Poppy Gould (12)
St Bernard's Convent School, Slough

Going To The Dentist

For how much longer will I be on the edge of my seat?
Waiting and waiting, sweating from the heat.
People go in and I don't see them come out,
It makes me wonder and makes me doubt,
If I'll still be alive when I come out.

The old receptionist calls out my name.
I smile at her happily but I'm dreading it all the same.
As you enter the room, it's filled with pictures of bright blue skies.
But I don't get fooled by that; it's really just a disguise.

The dentist is really there to make you scream and cry.
He loves to watch your pain and agony, you can see it in his eye.
Next comes the drill, it's like a snake, ready to strike at its prey.
'It won't hurt one bit!' So they say.

'Just lie back and relax,' he smiles at me.
'Oh, and did you have a nice holiday?' he adds with glee.
But I don't fall for the happy look
Or the questions, they're really just a hook

To make me forget all about the drill,
When what I'm feeling is closer to ill.

Finally the drill stops and you think it's all over - but it's not!
Because now comes the mouthwash and you have to gargle the lot.

And as I stumble on my way
The dentist gives me no sympathy, he just says, 'Good day!'

Caitlin Fawkes (12)
St Bernard's Convent School, Slough

The Trip Of A Lifetime

We're waiting, we're waiting
And we must not be late.
As today is the day
With a very important date!

We're laughing and joking,
We're running around.
Where is she? Where is she?
She must be found.

A-ha! Whoopee!
I'm so glad to see
The face of dear mother of mine.

Alas for me, her face seemed to be,
Completely upside down.
With her face not smiling and her rosy-red cheeks
not trying,
She seemed to have a frown.

'The car's broken and it cannot be fixed,
So sorry, we cannot go.'
Tears came to my eyes and my lips started to tremble,
A tantrum I was about to throw.

Sarah Duppa-Whyte (12)
St Bernard's Convent School, Slough

The Sunday Match

Football is a very competitive game,
Where the main objective is always the same.
You always want to be the best
Always better than the rest.
The strikers always want to score,
More and more and more and more!

The keeper likes to keep their sheet clean,
To prevent their manager from turning mean.
As the ball rolls to the keeper's feet,
The keeper's heart misses a beat.
But the striker gets there first,
It rustles the net. *Goal!*

Jordan Gray (12)
St Bernard's Convent School, Slough

Reggae Beat

The unbearable heat
The cool splash of the pool,
To not go to Jamaica
Would make you a fool.

As I struggle to keep up
With the reggae beat
I see them all smiling
As they quickly move their feet.

'Yeah Mon!' they say,
As they laugh to the sun,
They're never unhappy
Always seeming to have fun.

Terrible poverty,
Kids with bare feet
And yet they're still smiling
To the happy, reggae beat.

Grace Iglesias (13)
St Gabriel's School, Newbury

The Box Made Of My Heart

These are the things that I would put in my box,
Memories to be kept forever.
Some sad, some happy,
All for generations to learn from.

First thing in the morning,
The crisp sea air blowing on my face.
Sitting on the soft, white sand.
The waves tickling my toes.

My friends and family,
The moments, experiences and memories,
Shared with them all.
Joyful, playful, mourning and loss.

Those who look into my box will know
Like a friend looking deep into my eyes,
As if all my thoughts go to her.

Memories of when I was well and healthy,
Into my box, I would put
My last year and what it has brought me through.
Hoping this would prepare my children.

The first sight of lions
In Kenya, the open savannah.
So camouflaged against the dry grass,
So peaceful and lonely.

A box to keep all things precious in
For my children to see,
All the memories of my life,
Made from my heart.

Chantelle Rizan (12)
St Gabriel's School, Newbury

Superstition In Punjab

Step over a person?
It is bad luck for them,
Undo it! Go over again.

Your first new car?
What colour to choose?
Anything but black would be safe to use.

About to start a task?
But you sneeze. Oh no!
Stop! Abandon! Just go.

If your right eye twitches,
Something bad is due.
I should be careful of you.

Superstition in Punjab,
Is it real or not?
Just think about the consequences
It could cost you a lot!

Karanjeet Rai (13)
St Gabriel's School, Newbury

Siesta

Morning comes with sunrise,
In smiling, sapphire skies.
The sea rolls in, offering its abundant fruits,
That fishermen seek to pick.
A freshly cooked lunch will soon be ready,
Twists, turns and nautical themes is the theme for the meal.

Lunchtime arrives,
Followed by silence.
No one around,
Sun beaming down.
Harder
On the colourful terracotta floors
Free as siesta takes over.

Natasha Westbrook (13)
St Gabriel's School, Newbury

Different Ground

Travelling down a long, winding road
Driving far away from home
Village to town, so many sounds
It's not what I'm used to
It's different ground

Sunshine beaming through the trees
The pool rippling at my feet
Bright beaches invite me to see
Days growing longer
While each day grows hotter
It's not what I'm used to
It's different ground

People talking in a jumbled language
It's hard to understand them
In this strange land
I wander down the beach front
With a cool drink
Watching the orange sunset
It's not what I'm used to
It's different ground.

Imogen Collins (14)
St Gabriel's School, Newbury

Walkabout
(Inspired by the novel 'Walkabout')

'W arrigal' they shouted at me I didn't know what they were saying.
A borigines they were called, no one knew why.
L arana they called me, not knowing what their mission was.
K een to meet I was, but not so much anymore.
A ustralian outback was new to me.
B ut now I see what they really meant.
O ur lives had crossed, become entangled.
U nder, down under, was very different from home.
T he aborigines left my dream, it was a dream.

Nicholle Barnhill
St Gabriel's School, Newbury

The Spanish Market

Wandering down an overcrowded market,
Voices calling in the native tongue,
The sweet smell of fresh fruit and salty seafood,
Drifts by me in the warm breeze.

Bright colours flash around me,
Pinks, reds, blues, oranges and purples.
Of the people's clothes and fresh flowers
Everything is vibrant here.
Outside on the main street,
Another festival is taking place,
Loud music and enthusiastic dancers,
Line the streets in amazing and colourful costumes

Restaurants crowd the main street,
Plastic tables with colourful umbrellas,
Shielding from the hot, liquid sun,
People sit drinking Sangria,
Watching the world go by.

Everyone always heads for the coastal belt,
The sun, sea and sand,
But an equally beautiful place lies within
The rolling hills and beautiful orchards and vineyards,
Dotted with charming villages and ancient historic sights.

This is a place of many contrasts,
But here I feel at home.

Kate Robinson (13)
St Gabriel's School, Newbury

The Phoenix

Fulfilling a dream of memories both happy and sad
Is a trip to New York, a place of contrasts.

To some it's dirty, noisy, a place without pause
To reflect or recover.
It's brash but full of life
Yet a place of sadness.
Where the Twin Towers are no more,
Whose shadowy forms continue to frighten.

It's also a place of fashion, fun and festivity.
A never-ending cycle of
Movie stars,
Famous streets
And the Statue of Liberty.

A place of freedom which though affected by sadness
Will rise again from its ashes.

Catherine Ramsbottom (13)
St Gabriel's School, Newbury

My Old School

I used to go to school not very far away
I arrived at eight each morning and left at six each day.

My year had thirty children, most of whom were boys
What they lacked in manners they made up for in noise

Most girls would normally do their studies
The boys more often chat with buddies

But the boys were fun in their way
They added something to each day

The teachers made us try our best
Though from time to time we got a rest

But though I miss it, I really do
I'm very happy here, it's true.

Emma Clark (11)
St Gabriel's School, Newbury

Canarian Days

Every country different,
Every single little island,
Each has its own culture,
In its own unique way.

The hot Canary Islands,
Relaxing, peaceful, on the beach.
With the slow rolling and
Swishing of waves.

Travelling in a stuffy taxi,
Going down town for dinner,
Beeping horns,
People cursing in that foreign tongue.

Finally reaching the restaurant,
Hearing loud frying,
Sizzling dishes,
And chefs shouting.

Stuffed and feeling jolly
After a huge, traditional meal.
Wondering what to do next,
Seeing the flashing lights,
Knowing what to do next.

Ready for a late night shop,
Strolling down the street,
Taking in the ka-ching of tills,
And sliding of hangers on rails.

Loitering back to the hotel,
Listening to the clicking crickets,
And humming lizards
The moonlight shining off the splashing pool.

Slowly opening my eyes,
Another bright, refreshing Canarian day.

Rachel Phillips (13)
St Gabriel's School, Newbury

Nerja Market

A Nerja market,
Let's set the scene,
Where children shout,
And banners stream.

Standing alone,
With hands at my sides,
Streets filled with stalls,
And unusual cries.

A sea of people surge ahead,
An empty town stands behind.
Engulfed in the smell of roasted nuts,
Screaming children,
And sceptical 'tuts'
Angry locals shoot indignant stares,
At ecstatic tourists who shouldn't be there.

My feet drag as the sun breathes,
A heavy sigh of sweltering heat,
My head burns,
My face sweats,
Swallowed by the humidity,
Gasping for breath.

I see the exit,
The curtains
I'm coming to the end
I'm back into the streets of Nerja,
Another market ends.

Holly Woodhead (13)
St Gabriel's School, Newbury

During The Day, During The Night

During the day:

Dazzling sun beats across my forehead
Like a cloak of warmth, spread around me,
A swoop of wind pulls my hair to one side
And I see the calm sea.

Noise is quietened as I turn to the streets,
To see dancing colours of light.
Darting from door to door, street to street,
As I focus I see cheery faces
And lightly coated demerara skin.

The sun goes higher,
And people come into view,
Side alleys, streets even shop doorways
Are crammed with stalls of mouth-watering,
Colourful foods, of all shapes and sizes.

The smell makes your nostrils flair
And your tastebuds swell with delight.
For exotica is its name, exotic is its game!

At night:

A deep and twinkled blanket of night,
Covers my eyes.
Everything is still.
Waters are calm and sweet.
Ripples are few but they remain in view.
Underneath the beams of twinkling light,
From the great splodge of grey paint among the twinkles.

I heave the sacks above my eyes,
Down towards the street,
Where the delightful smell
Remains amongst the dayless air!

Kate Langley-Smith (13)
St Gabriel's School, Newbury

Cradled In The Arms Of Love

Sweet dreams my child, let your innocent eyes rest
May the angels carry you for you deserve the best,
May God hold you in his hands and dance with you in your heart
May we be together and never part.

Paradise follows you whether you may go
Beyond the heavens, where the waterfalls flow,
As clear as the dewdrops, the Queen Fairy herself
Comes to comfort when you need the world's help.

The night will come when your eyes begin to close
The angels are white because it's the colour you chose,
The nightingale sings when only you can hear
God is on standby to wipe away every tear.

So sleep my child, upon the wings of love
Let Cupid guide you on your journey above,
Hear the whispers of princesses of heroines before
For they will cradle you when you fall.

Your love allows the angels to fly,
The tides to turn, the sun to rise.
Your tears fill the sea, which hide your pain
Beyond the unknown depths on the runaway train.

Lay your head upon the petal of a rose
Let the statues take their final pose
Close your eyes and safely dream
Your secret's safe between you and me.

Georgina Le Flufy (15)
St Gabriel's School, Newbury

The Morning Island

Morning.
The calming waves break,
Golden sun
Beaming down
On the small, deserted beach.

Happy
Summer visitors
Taking in
Breath-taking
Mediterranean views.

Hear the
Laughter, laughter
From the children in the warm sea,
Playing among colourful fish

Another beautiful day.

Katie Bourne (13)
St Gabriel's School, Newbury

Water

Dripping from the tap,
Flowing from the river,
Falling from the waterfall
Gushing down the streams,
Rolling, rushing, running,
Water everywhere.
Sweeping up the pebbles,
Carrying them away.
Waves roaring, riding,
The enormous deep blue sea,
Filling every gap they can,
Rippling in the breeze.

Clare Warwick (11)
St Gabriel's School, Newbury

Illusions

A flicker of light. a flash of the hand,
And quickly, the cards are dealt.
The magician's very clever, messing with your head,
You look away for a second and he's laid the perfect spread.

You think that magic is taking place
It's exciting and it's fun,
But when you think the trick's happening
Sorry, it's already been done.

Illusions are what we thrive on,
Playing mess-games with our minds,
We love them, we watch them, we live them
All sorts of different kinds!

What's love but an illusion?
What's joy, what's sorrow and pain?
The whole world's our illusion,
We are all just playing the game!

Chantelle Davison (13)
St Gabriel's School, Newbury

Island Life

Fish market bustles
Church bells lie dormant until Sunday,
Sea washes up onto the pink and white sand,
The faint murmuring of ploughs in the sugarcane fields,
Humming in the sparkling distance,
Clicking of cameras as the beaches fill with black, white and red.
The smell of fish wafts through the sweltering air,
Bells of the ice cream man
Followed by delighted screams of children still in school uniform,
Released to a freedom in the sun.

Naomi Rowe-Gurney (13)
St Gabriel's School, Newbury

The Show Ring

The frantic final grooming,
As the judge enters the ring,
Then the steward gives the signal
For the showing to begin.

Ponies push and shove,
To gain their rightful place,
As their jockeys do not smile,
They all are stony-faced.

The judge continues watching,
Through the trot and canter too,
As the ponies show extension
And the mothers start to *coo!*

After the shows are all complete,
The tension starts to rise,
Everyone is waiting
To see who gains the prize.

The loudspeaker gives a crack,
And then a high-pitched squeak.
A pony gives a little buck,
A mother gives a shriek.

The little buck turns to a rear,
And another pony bolts,
A madly frantic parent,
Can only wait and hope.

Ponies charging round the ring,
The judge dodges a bay,
Only to be mowed over
By a pony the other way.

The frantic steward gives a nod,
And all ponies start to go.
One girl starts shrieking,
Her pony has lost a bow.

The commentator's flattened,
The sponsor looks quite dead.
The mothers all take up a vow
To compete at knitting instead.

Hannah Windmill (13)
St Gabriel's School, Newbury

Myalgic Encephalomyelitis

M y illness is long
Y esterday, today
A ll the same
L ong sometimes hard
G rowing pains in my legs
I ncreasing tiredness
C ritical I stay positive.

E ndurance is the key
N ot always I have too
C omes and goes it does
E ither life is hard or sometimes it is like the olden times
P hysically well I was, until . . .
H ammering down on me like
A load of rain.
L ike all chronic illnesses we learn to get through
O nly life is different now
M ore challenging
Y ou learn to understand your body
E very sign, you
L earn when to stop to rest.
I f I were to ignore these signs now I am ill
T hen I would become more sick,
I now can understand and manage my chronic illness
S oon (I hope) I'll be better.

Charlotte Garner (11)
St Gabriel's School, Newbury

Alone

I called and called
But could not hear
Not a single sound
Fell upon my ear.

Where were you
When I was so afraid?
I looked for you
You should have stayed!

A knock at the door
A creaking stair
A dripping tap
But you weren't there.

All alone,
Didn't you care?
Under the bed you hid
My long-lost teddy bear!

Angharad Evans (14)
St Gabriel's School, Newbury

Flat Fields Of Blood

The hot, grainy sand shifts and moves,
Rocks stand out over the golden sea.
Natural and sharply defined,
Fire flame-red, yellow and orange,
These colours strong, bold and harsh,
Flat fields of blood
Sweat-plastered gully,
All pervading heat,
Upon the hot, burning surface.
Those lonely footsteps, walking
As the Aborigine continued his trail.

Charlotte Davies (13)
St Gabriel's School, Newbury

Memories In A Box

My box of memories,
Not an ordinary box,
But one that will stay in mind forever.
Memories of family in my head,
Reunions, weddings and funerals.
The saddest part is saying goodbye.

The Elgar cello concerto singing in my ears.
The sight of an orchestra and sounds of the cello.
'YoYo Ma' sways as he plays,
Music fills the concert hall.
Maybe it will never end,
But everything does eventually.

The sights of magnificent cathedrals
From all around the world.
The Sagrada Familia, with its glorious towers,
Shimmering in the Barcelona sunlight.
Saint Peter's in Rome with its huge dome,
The frail Pope sits on his throne
Watching the huge crowd below.

Rosaleen Morshead (12)
St Gabriel's School, Newbury

Autumn Fall

Conkers swelling in their silk-lined shells then plummet to the ground.
The oak trees expel their acorns and squirrels receive them.
Leaves drift to the ground, orange, yellow, brown.
Early frosts sparkle like jewels.
Pumpkins ripen and are ready to be hollowed out.
Bonfires crackle and the smell of wood smoke fills the air,
The clocks fall back, this is autumn.

Imogen West (12)
St Gabriel's School, Newbury

Storm

I see Storm come in his black chariot
Pulled by hounds which race like mad wolves.
In his right arm he holds
A tray full of night clouds
Which he scatters here and there.
The clouds are in chaos;
Who must go where?
But when Storm does shout,
Order prevails and his voice is heard clearly.
Storm thunders and growls,
He fumes and he roars
He wakes up the sea.

Her beauty appeases him,
He comes down to her
To play and to dance with her.
Water, the sweet one, dances for them:
Lapping at the bow of the fair ship,
Or sending one tossing high;
Sending one diving down low, yet
Never letting it sink.

Now Storm remembers his son Wind,
He rushes up to him in joy
So together they go to their work.
Pulling at pretty girls' hair
Sending their skirts billowing like sails
Pushing at umbrellas and sending newspapers scuttling.
But when Sir Sun appears -
Storm and his clouds just flee.

Myriam Frenkel (13)
St Gabriel's School, Newbury

The Old Man

I saw an old man
With a snowy-white beard
That seemed to touch the ground.
His eyebrows were clouds
And his teeth all sticky,
Covered in yellow paint.
His grey, check hat, down,
A black face on the front,
With the price on the side.
With lead-pencilled hair
Sticking out at the sides
With a touch of bright white.
His coat all hunched up
With his black collar up,
Covering up his face
With filthy, brown shoes
Covered with mucky mud
Like the frown on his face.
He then looked at me
Seeing me studying him -
Up and down, round and round.
He gave me a look, I think it was a smile,
But then I said goodbye,
'Goodbye, my old man!'

Kimberley Taylor (12)
St Gabriel's School, Newbury

My Beach

Around me the clear turquoise sea.
Between my toes the clean white sand oozes.
The sound of the gentle waves lapping the shore
One hammock sways in the soft breeze.
The dolphins and multicoloured fish are playing
Happily in the ocean.
The palm trees are moving in the breeze.
There's one sailing boat with pure white sails
Drifting in the sea without a sound.
Straw umbrellas dotted along the beach casting a crazy shadow.
Barbecues roasting slowly, fill the air with delicious smells.
While fires crackle invitingly, in the distance a whale spouting
Past a vast stretch of coral reef near to the shore.
The sea's warmth beckons invitingly,
Stretching into an unknown distance.
The sun's glittering rays bake my skin.
The beach is calm and deserted except for my family.
The beach is too nice to have a name.
My beach is paradise.

Bethan Rudgley (11)
St Gabriel's School, Newbury

Eclipse

A bulb that is turned on, then off,
A candle snuffed out with a breath of wind.
A midsummer's day with a black-out,
A short night in the middle of the day.
A blinding light illuminating the sky.
The hooting of the owl as the clock strikes noon,
As the light vanishes, bats appear,
A few seconds of darkness.

Leah Vellam-Steptoe (12)
St Gabriel's School, Newbury

Fashion

Fashion is like an endless cycle
With trends that come and go
People get sucked in with shopping fever
They can't resist
The latest styles
It's like a disease!
People spend, spend, spend!

You love it or you hate it
One season's must-have's are . . .
Pinks, purples, baggy jeans and platforms
Give way to next season's spending spree which are . . .
Bright colours, short skirts and stilettos
It's crazy!
People spend, spend, spend!

Fashion is like a hungry dog
But hungry for money
One season's must-have's
Are next season's cast-off's
Always changing
You must keep up!
People spend, spend, spend!

Adults like to spend their money on
Expensive Gucci and Chanel
Whilst kids go cheap
On New Look and Tammy
Those with more money
Go to surf shops
Like Quicksilver and Roxy
People, spend, spend, spend!

Jennie Gillam (12)
St Gabriel's School, Newbury

My Box Of Many Memories

My box has strong sides built over
Many years with my memories.
It is filled with my senses,
My feelings and emotions.

The smell of patisseries wafts out of it.
The bitter coffee and sweet croissants mingle together,
Along with freshly baked baguettes.

In my box I glide over the sea in a boat,
Like an iron over silk, smoothing out the creases,
The warm water splashing gently.

The sound of a baby gurgling can be heard.
My brother, his tiny arms and legs waving in the air,
With a look of innocent curiosity on his delicate face.

The distant chants from a mosque break the silence
Of the morning, echoing through the empty streets,
As the sun begins to light a new day.

Her soft fur runs through my fingers, as I feel inside my box,
While my cat purrs softly, tilting her head to the side
As I gently stroke her velvet coat.

The Land Rover skids across the sand, as the grit flies
Into the air, hitting the dunes that we have just climbed
And accelerating as we ascend another.

I bend into my box and smell the sweet aroma
Of the frangipanis, like a sugary syrup,
With the flower's white petals glistening in the bright sun.

These are the contents of my box, not yet full,
Ready to hold many more of my memories,
So one day I may look back and remember.

Kirsten Riddick (12)
St Gabriel's School, Newbury

A Place To Store My Happiness

My box is made of glass,
Clear so everyone can see in it,
So they can see all my memories.
My box is full of happiness,
No tears, fear or hatred.

My family are everything,
Providing help and guidance
Providing a home
A warm home where I am always happy.

My bed, soft and squishy, warm and comforting.
A place where I can shed my tears alone.

On my bed sits snowman
A teddy, old and dirty that shows many memories.
Yellow from the soap I tried to clean him with
And brown from being outside.

The chilling air whipping my cheeks,
Warm sun beating on my back
The refreshing ski runs, the tiresome walks.
The wonder works called the mountains.

The cheery chatter, the warmth surrounding
A second family is found at St Gabriel's.

The crispy chips with mountains of mayonnaise,
Soft sand and the crashing waves.
Sand in my bed and sand in my toes,
Months spent at the Belgian coast.

The soft sounds and the high-pitched squeaks,
The happy playing and the nerve-wracking concerts.
Music is everywhere.

So in my box my memories go,
Full of happiness, no fears or tears.

Emilie Atkinson (12)
St Gabriel's School, Newbury

My Box Of Memories

In my box, made out of the love and care for my family and friends,
I have:
The sweet, burning scent of raging bonfires on a cold winter night.
The desperate cry of a lonely guinea pig
lost forever without its soulmate.
The soft, soothing, silky fur of my hamster
and its cute, intelligent eyes staring at me after a long day's work.
The sight of a beautiful, powerful stallion
tearing through the grass like a speeding cheetah.
The colours of a setting sun, glowing down from the magnificent sky.
A cold winter morning, the sun beaming at me
from the cold, blue sky and the snow crunching underneath my feet
as I make those first footsteps in a white world.
A day out to the sea, the sand blowing underneath me
and the waves rippling at my feet.
My box of memories is one that I will treasure forever
because one day somebody else will treasure this box as I did today.

Catherine Page (12)
St Gabriel's School, Newbury

The Truth Of The Beach

The beach huts stood stiffly on guard
standing sentinel on the sandy shore;
Children ran in and out exploring the mysterious caves
With thousands of eyes
Staring down at them from the ceiling.

Paragliders have a bird's eye view of the rainbow-coloured dominoes
lined up idly, fighting for every inch of space.
Seagulls screeching, pleasing the bird watchers
As they turn their heads up and gaze.

The white surf overlapping the incoming waves like a sea horse
proudly flicking its mane.
As the beach becomes empty the noise subsides
But not everyone has gone because underneath
the seabed life has just begun.

Rebecca Mason (11)
St Gabriel's School, Newbury

My Box Of Wonderful Things

My box of wonderful things,
Would be made from all the occasions
I choose to remember.
Strung together like a patchwork quilt
Made from a photo album.
I would keep in it oceans on which I could set my sails
Or paddle into the rays of glowing sunshine
Rippling off the waves;
Sunshine to brighten up a tired day
With golden light from out of this world,
Heat shooting down to warm my back on a cold winter's day.
I'd keep laughter sounding so bubbling and full,
Exploding over the universe.
I would keep the smell of gardens
Wet after the rain.
And an array of flowers sprayed with dew,
Newly mown grass after a shower.
I would treasure the memories,
Of my family at happy occasions
Every time I close the lid.

Charlotte Weeks (12)
St Gabriel's School, Newbury

My Holiday Beach

Battered boats bobbed along the crystal sea
As the palm trees swayed in the breeze
Seagulls screeched loudly in the sunset
White sand oozed between my toes
As the sun shone brightly down.
Splashing and yelling with glee
My brothers played in the sea
On my beach perfect
It is perfect.

Charlotte Jordan (11)
St Gabriel's School, Newbury

Dreams Can Come True

This is my story . . .
I was a little princess in a terrible mess,
Ruled a kingdom alone where no love was confessed,
I dreamed of a prince on a tall, white horse,
I ran like a spirit to surrender to this force.

My people would say this night and day,
'This prince can't be real; there is no way,
Why won't she just forget this dream?
What does she think it all will mean?'

'He seems to be deep in the royal heart,
She cries at night, she doesn't want to be apart.
Prince, oh prince, are you really sincere?
I'll bet you one day she's going to disappear.'

The morning, it changed, was crystal and cold,
I was in my chamber when I was told,
'There's a prince outside and he's calling your name,
The one from your dreams, oh the very same.'

I ran below and fell into his arms
Now he protects me from any harm.
Listen to my story through and through
And let me prove that dreams can come true.

Sophie Totten (12)
St Gabriel's School, Newbury

My Perfect Beach

Clear, warm blue sea reflects the glittering sun that looks down from
Bright blue skies without a cloud in sight.

Gentle lapping waves kiss the bottom of drifting sailing boats
While underneath are brightly coloured fish dodging about
Few people are sunbathing on the golden fine sand.

The salty flavours in the air tingle on my tongue,
Games, races, competitions, amazing sandcastles and picnics
Were held there, all held at this beach of family outings.

Olivia McCarthy (11)
St Gabriel's School, Newbury

The Owl

Flying through the sacred night
A solitary moonlight figure
Gliding swiftly on and on
Beneath the sparkling stars

His eyes like fearsome golden globes
Full of knowledge and wisdom
Searching through the endless black
For poor, helpless prey

His talons sharp as a butcher's knife
Carved and powerful too
His beak hooked and pointed
Ready to attack and kill

His keen eyes spot an innocent vole
Unaware of the danger
The predator swoops quickly in
To claim his well-earned prize.

Charlotte Horner (12)
St Gabriel's School, Newbury

Seaside

It was a lovely day.
We skipped on the soft sand.
We dipped our feet in the icy waves.
We watched the sea horses bobbing
Around like those on a merry-go-round.
The scorching sun glistened on the sparkling sea
Like diamonds, a blue background.
Rocks tumbled over each other
In various shapes and sizes.
A sudden gust of wind whipped
Two surfers over and brought in a load of
Seaweed with them.

Becky Westall (11)
St Gabriel's School, Newbury

The Darkness Crept . . .

(Inspired by the novel 'Walkabout')

The powdery blackness ebbed into my soul.
It was a friendly enemy.
It forever loomed over me,
As if frozen,
Lulling in lost dreams,
It awkwardly wriggled.
The blotchy opaqueness
Froze my soul,
Shrivelled my hopes
And made me a stranger to myself.
As the anguish of unwanted darkness
Drove its havoc and chaos,
Deep into my innocence,
I watched the mesmerising figures,
Dancing on the horizon.
Paranoia had exhausted me,
But the glorious sun
Displayed its colours.
I could finally feel my heart beat regularly.
I inquisitively explored my surroundings,
But still not another friendly species such as I.
You may be unique and individual,
But here,
You're just another shape under the sun.

Lorna Fisher (14)
St Gabriel's School, Newbury

My Special Box

My box is full of sights and sounds,
Memories, hopes and dreams,
My laughter and my sadness
And my friends and family.

The gentle lapping of water,
On the shore of an empty beach.
The autumn leaves that fall
On the grass in the morning sun.

My brother's hockey matches
And watching him play,
Following in his footsteps
As I do the same.

Playing in the garden,
Having waterfights with Dad,
Then relaxing in a deck chair with Mum,
Deep in my latest book.

Jumping into the pool,
To be the first one to get in,
The ripples and the splash,
The sense of utter freedom.

All these things, pieced together like patchwork,
Make me who I am.
And I know that they will always be there,
Whenever I open the lid . . .

Lucy Peacock (12)
St Gabriel's School, Newbury

The Beach

As the red sun melts into the
deep blue sea leaving a
distant glow in the orange sky;

The dolphins are leaping out in the
turquoise blue;

The palm trees rustle in
the gentle breeze;

The waves lap onto the
glittering white sand;

A swinging hammock is swaying
in the breeze.

The slow-burning fire made out of
old, dry palm leaves crackled
and licked at the fish I had caught.

This beach was deserted.

Rebecca Steljes (11)
St Gabriel's School, Newbury

Darkness

(Inspired by the novel 'Walkabout')

The blackness getting deeper
So many people fast asleep
Dreaming of many dreams
The rabbit's foot heavily beating on the ground.

Fireflies flickering in the blank sky
The bobcat's sneakily slunk away
Up in a tree an owl sat so bright-eyed
The night so bland.

Soon it was near sunrise
Dewdrops began to settle on the grass
The sun was rising now
How weird that night had been.

Carmilla Deas (13)
St Gabriel's School, Newbury

The Sparkling Night

Crescent moon motionless,
Gently rising
A hazeless light.
Well-shaded ghost,
The spirit of death
Floating in the water.

Sparkling night lights,
In the darkness
Shadowing the trees.
Smoke drifts across the stars,
In the darkness like a
Snake slithering silently.

Shattered glass across,
The dark, swivelling path
Dazzling like jewels.
Cool pools,
Of glittering silver
In the shadows.
As the moonstones
Sparkle in the rocks.

Olivia Derwent (14)
St Gabriel's School, Newbury

My Holiday Beach

Golden, boiling sand burnt my hesitant feet.
Multicoloured windbreaks protected lunch boxes.
Fun, screams of little children were lost in the noise.
The turquoise sea breaking as I speak.
With waves so big they exploded at my feet.
Speedboats were zooming across the open sea.
White, enormous sea horses tossed their manes.

Polly London (11)
St Gabriel's School, Newbury

The Changing Beach

The sea laps at the harbour wall
The seaweed attaches itself to all things near
Greens and blues all mixed in the waves
The sun shines bright over the glistening beach
Pure white sand in strong, proud sandcastles
Deckchairs in red and white stripes
Umbrellas cover warm, brown bodies
The sea calm and quiet
Then mist creeps over the sun
The sky becomes dark
The people disappear
The chairs vanish
The clear sea becomes deeper and darker
The wind now cold and stinging
The waves roll fiercely, all mighty and strong
The once proud sandcastles flattened
The tide is rising
The sea claims the seaweed back
To where it first came from
The waves no longer lap, but crash and roll on the harbour
The beach is transformed
No place to be this afternoon.

Lucy Varman (12)
St Gabriel's School, Newbury

My Beach Poem!

Palm trees swaying like washing on the line,
Waves gently lapping over the turquoise sea
Coloured glass glistening like jewels in the sparkly sun.
Jet skis bouncing up and down in the distance
Dolphins and turtles diving like an arrow to the ocean floor,
Fresh fruit salad the servants are bringing
Cabaret music and Caribbean singing,
Complete a wonderful picture.

Emma Hellewell (11)
St Gabriel's School, Newbury

No Idea

I don't know what to write about
This is too hard without a doubt
I could write about the classroom wall
No, that would make no sense at all

I don't know what to write about
This is too hard without a doubt
I could write about the ceiling high
No, that is so boring it would make people sigh

I don't know what to write about
This is too hard without a doubt
I could write about the clock, telling the time
No, that would be the dullest ever rhyme

I don't know what to write about
This is too hard without a doubt
What to write, oh I don't know
So long, farewell, I've got to go!

Stephanie Wall (11)
St Gabriel's School, Newbury

My Holiday Beach

There are only a few people on the golden sand,
They stare out over the glittering turquoise sea.
The quiet is broken by the jet skis and seagulls screeching.
Baking skin is shaded by the swaying palm trees,
Cool waves lapping at hot feet.
Children screaming with joy,
Braided heads bobbing in the sea,
Smiles as wide as the scenery.

Juliette Broadbridge (11)
St Gabriel's School, Newbury

My Beach Poem

Waves throw themselves carelessly
Against the slippery, green rocks,
Children darting around
Chasing each other in a game,
People smiling as I run by them,
Cold, I run to my spot on the beach,
Reaching for my towel after an icy dip in the sea,
Other people's excitement was catching,
Yummy hot dogs from the beach cafe
Make my tummy grumble.
The sun cooks my body
As I lie there on my towel,
Waves gently lapping
Over the soft sand
That burns my baking feet
The glistening sea disappears
Into a hazy distance.

Phoebe Smyth (11)
St Gabriel's School, Newbury

City Scene

C hildren chatter in busy places
I nquisitive inspectors inspect schools
T axis trek through crowded streets
Y elling children cry for help.

S hoe shops selling stiletto shoes
C ats calling on city corners
E lectricians eagerly execute their daily job
N ewspapers, newspapers fresh off the press
E lectric lights are eccentric.

Abigail Oakton (11)
St Gabriel's School, Newbury

In The Christmas Box

My box is made of snowflakes,
Dancing in the winter nights.
It is also made of delight and happiness,
To finish it to the touch.
In the snow on a cold winter's morning,
The first to place your footprints.
Far in the distance, you see warm spirits,
As children make angels in the snow.
The faces of young ones on Christmas Day,
All full of curiosity, excitement, smiles,
Fighting over what tinsel, which baubles.
The proud moment when the angel is up.
Listening to the man in the family
Trying to show you how to sing old carols.
Exhausted little faces, ice fingers,
When they roll the cold ball of snow around,
Reaching up to make the snowman complete,
With the eyes, nose, hat and scarf.
Setting fire to the figgy pudding,
Adding brandy butter to the mince pies.
Pulling open the crackers with suspense
To see what awaits them this year!
Keeping forever these memories of
Pearly-white and treasured gold.
In this box they'll stay
Until Christmas comes again.

Amy Keenan (12)
St Gabriel's School, Newbury

Dolphin Song

I walked along the endless causeway,
My mind somewhere different,
I looked over the glistening sea waves,
My eyes dreaming although they shouldn't

The air was moist,
The smell was clear,
The dolphin song was very near.

I gathered my thoughts and stood up straight,
I then sung out my rightful song,
The dolphin came, he is never late,
He flicked his tail and he was gone.

The air was moist,
The smell was clear,
The dolphin song was very near.

I heard his lovely, harmonious tune,
I saw him in the light.
He then jumped up as high as the moon,
I wished his friend was all right.

The air was moist,
The smell was clear,
The dolphin song was very near.

Pollution is around, you just don't know,
It is quicker to kill than an arrow and bow,
So take care of the world, take care of the sea,
Open the prison of pollution and set wildlife free.

Esme Bennett (12)
St Gabriel's School, Newbury

Sadness

Sadness.
A tightening inside,
That you can't get rid of.

Sadness.
A tear trying to hide,
That you can't see, but feel.

Sadness.
A regret of selfishness,
That you can't take back.

Sadness.
A feeling of unhappiness,
That you can't disguise.

Sadness.
A journey,
That is never-ending!

Bethany Hensman (12)
St Gabriel's School, Newbury

The Cat

The cat for evermore
Sits assembled by the front door,
He creeps silently down the lawn
And his tail wafts through the corn,
Mostly sleeping
And sometimes preening,
But always waiting . . .
With one eye open
For the desolate shadow
of the mouse
next door.

Sophie Davis (12)
St Gabriel's School, Newbury

Dance

Sways, turns, jumps and kicks
Steps, hops, splits and flicks

Twirling, whirling, spinning around
In perfect time with the music's sound.

Finally a finishing pose which I held
From the top of my head to the tips of my toes.

Clapping, cheering, jeering and shouting.
It was only myself I was doubting.

Third place, second place, the both had gone.
Little did I know that I had won.

I was awarded a trophy that was made of solid gold
It was nearly too heavy for me to hold.

On the way home from me you heard not even a peep
After such an eventful day I fell straight to sleep.

Nicola Bates (12)
St Gabriel's School, Newbury

A Day At The Seaside

The glistening reflection on the rippling sea,
Makes the early morning fishermen smile with glee.

The children arrive with their buckets and spades,
While the parents sunbathe with suncream and shades.

The kiddies run riot with their ice cream and sweets,
As they paddle in the sea with their rough, sandy feet.

The sun skims the sea and the fishermen draw near,
The sea starts to roughen as the people can hear.

The seagulls glide low searching for food,
Left by the families as the day concludes.

Sophie Holland (12)
St Gabriel's School, Newbury

Money Cannot Buy Happiness

Everyone wants to be popular
Never to be seen alone
Have all the right clothes and make-up
And the most expensive phone.

To be one of the popular ones
Who everyone wants to be
But behind all that make-up
Is a different personality.

To go on lots of holidays
Have a house with a swimming pool
Be surrounded by 'real friends'
And have no worries at all.

But those so-called 'real friends'
May desert you one day
Money cannot buy happiness
Whatever people may say.

Bronwen Edwards (13)
St Gabriel's School, Newbury

In My Box . . .

In my box carved from memories
I will put all the things that mean a lot to me,
The smell of golden chips crackling and bubbling in a pan,
The sound of people laughing, knowing that they are having fun,
The feel of suede lightly touching my fingertips,
The memory of birthdays, the happy laughter,
The sound of paper crunching, being screwed up,
The look of glitter, shiny, light-catching and totally harmless,
The excitement of a football match, the buzz of walking in,
My team scoring and jumping up and down to celebrate,
In my box these memories, smells, excitement, looks and touch,
All these things make my box
And my box carved from memories makes me.

Alex Sharp (12)
St Gabriel's School, Newbury

Inferior

She's far to busy,
She won't even bother,
Why do I always
Get compared to my brother?

He would have done this,
He would have said that,
Well I'm nothing like him,
I don't do that.

I tried so hard to do it,
Haven't I done enough?
I can't do any better,
Life is far too tough.

She said I could do better,
I told her what I thought
She said I was a brat,
I don't want to be taught.

Rachel Broadbridge (13)
St Gabriel's School, Newbury

The Sound Of The Rainforest

The lime-green of the great canopy,
See the vines squirming like snakes, falling from above.
The rose-pink of the hummingbird's collar,
It sparkles like a diamond, given in deepest love.
The shimmering, golden yellow of the sun,
Lighting the world below, where the shadows lie.
The vibrant autumn-red of the scarlet macaw's feathers,
Flying like arrows across the violet-setting sky.
The clear, clear blue of Angel Falls' waters,
Cascading down the jagged, steep cliff wall.
The rich, fruity orange of the howler monkey's fur,
It leaps from branch to branch, screaming its persistent call.

Helen Broadbridge (11)
St Gabriel's School, Newbury

Animal Echoes

Purr of a cat,
So loyal and true.
Bark of a dog,
Scares me and you too!

Twitch of a rabbit,
So sudden and still.
Snarl of a fox,
Ready to kill!

Song of a nightingale,
So gentle and sweet.
Roar of a lion,
In the jungle heat!

Silence of a spider,
Sitting there all day.
Squeak of a mouse,
Hiding in the hay!

All the animals,
That I have ever heard.
Are special to me
And to our world!

Francesca Robertson (11)
St Gabriel's School, Newbury

Polar Bears

P ure, strong, fur crisp and white,
O n its own in the dawning night,
L iquid water moving in the distance,
A lonesome figure, waiting for a chance,
R eaching out towards the sun.

B efore the day has been and gone,
E verlasting darkness creeps forward,
A pure, crisp, white blanket - it's snow,
R eflecting in the evening glow.

Lucy Cannings (12)
St Gabriel's School, Newbury

Two Boys

In two different places,
Two boys are crying,
The first one's upset,
He just wants a pet.
He's asked very nicely,
Been very good,
He's still not allowed one,
Even though he should.

Now onto the next one,
He's very weak,
Been slapped by his mum,
Right on the cheek,
Starved by his stepfather,
He wants to have fun,
Is he what his mother says
Luckier than some?

Kirsten Williams (11)
St Gabriel's School, Newbury

The Doll

She sat alone in the corner, cobwebs covering her eyes
the frozen tear, glazing her fears
her shrunken clothes, tired and tried

Her fingers numb with the pain
the love stained on her faded cheeks
she knew it would never be the same

Her knees torn and stretched with the play
her smile disguising the truth
her hate like the shadows of the closing day.

Pippa Boyd (15)
St Gabriel's School, Newbury

As The Days Go By

I miss you every second and more every day,
With every part of my heart and breath I take.
I miss not being able to look in your eyes,
I miss you so much and I can't explain why.

I miss not telling you when things go wrong,
I miss the comfort you've given me for so long.
I miss not speaking to you over the phone,
Not hearing your voice and feeling so alone.

I miss not feeling your body close to mine,
When we breathed our hearts would beat in time.
I miss not waking up to you when morning comes,
I miss the little things that made us one.

I hate realising as the days go on,
That my reason for living this life has gone.
I hate the emptiness I feel inside,
You're the memory I can't re-write.

Rebecca Le Flufy (13)
St Gabriel's School, Newbury

Spring

The warm, sweet-smelling breath of wind,
As fresh as new sprung flowers,
So fresh as though they had just been born
From a mother's womb.

The newly born young, bleating,
Like newborn babies crying.
As tiny as a ball of wool,
That your eyes could be mistaken.

The first blades of grass,
Like the first people on Earth,
Is one of the signs that shows,
That spring is on its way.

Rachel Johnston (12)
St Gabriel's School, Newbury

The Bend Of A Street Corner

Punks peer round street corners
With their rings through their noses sparkling in the sunlight.
Blonde hair dipped in red, sticking up on end,
It's enough to give anybody a fright going round . . .
      the bend of a street corner!

A black cat comes round the street corner
With its green eyes glaring at me!
Its fur is sticking up on end,
I wouldn't like to meet that cat coming around . . .
      the bend of a street corner!

A runner runs round the street corner
Sweat running down his face.
They must be having a race,
I wouldn't like to meet them coming around . . .
      the bend of a street corner!

A £20 note comes flying round the street corner
The Queen's face,
Portrait-like, staring at me!
Now, I would like to meet this £20 note flying around . . .
      the bend of a street corner!

Camilla Gauntlett (12)
St Gabriel's School, Newbury

Bliss

The gentle breeze whipping through my hair,
Lying here in my secret lair,
The sun's rays heating my skin,
As I gaze at the paradise I am in.

The wave's hand lapping the sand,
An occasional sway of the palms so grand,
Lying here in undying harmony,
I realise that the only thing that could disconcert myself is me.

Emma Bailey (12)
St Gabriel's School, Newbury

A Day At The Seaside

'Get up! Get up!' my mother calls,
I run downstairs and across the hall.
'Get in the car and put on your belts,'
And off we drove at full pelt!

My brother is shouting in my ear,
I'm trying to get some sleep in here!
Over the hills and past huge cities,
There is traffic on the road, oh what a pity!

At last we are here at the beautiful sea,
My brother runs down the bank and scrapes his knee.
'Revenge,' I said quietly to myself,
Running down the bank trying not to hurt myself!

I quickly lay my brother down
And buried him in the sand.
He started wailing and whining,
On boiling hot sand as the sun was shining.

We ran into the sea and jumped the waves,
Oh this is one of the best summer holiday days!

The sun goes down and we all go home,
As I am eating an ice cream cone.
We say goodbye to the waves and sand,
Oh what a lovely summer holiday day that wasn't planned!

Rachel Knight (11)
St Gabriel's School, Newbury

Pandas At Play

Fluffy bears, black and white,
The colour of dominoes.
Standing out in the morning light,
Crunching on fresh bamboo,
The cubs are eating too.
Playing in the soft white snow
Tumbling, rolling in the sun's bright glow.

Georgina Carlisle (12)
St Gabriel's School, Newbury

Hallowe'en

It's the 31st of October, do you know what that means?
We run from door to door, 'Trick or treat? Trick or treat?'
Old ladies answer the door and give us a packet of sweets!
Witches, devils, ghosts too - the whole lot are coming so, 'Boo!'
Everybody's dressed up; the devils have their tridents.
The witches have their cauldrons and of course
The ghosts have their white bodies.
We go outside and play hide-and-seek in the dark!
'Stop! I heard a scream!'
We all run inside, scared out of our wits,
Mum has prepared a feast!
We dig into vampire's blood and witches' cat's eyes!
For pudding it's rats' tail pies!
It's getting late so we go and get into our pyjamas
And stay up late telling ghost stories about vampires
And wicked old women!

Elizabeth James-Crook (12)
St Gabriel's School, Newbury

The Faery Queen

She wears the white tunic of purity,
The blue cloak of spiritual aspiration
And the silver mask of the moon's intuition
As she holds the sword of freedom.

A leap of faith into a brighter future
As she soars in the sun's last rays.
Her wings are the swiftness of thought
And white stars glow where her feet have trod
As she dances and dwells in the twilight of dreams.

She awakens our sleeping potential with her sharp gaze
Poised at the crossroads of our lives,
Speaking in riddles, knowing what lies in wait for us all.
Her ethereal form floats through lives,
Enchanting their inner souls as she glides, for evermore.

Alice French (13)
St Gabriel's School, Newbury

Cold Winter Months

I love the cold winter months.
Wrapping up warm so we're snug as bugs.
Throwing snowballs and having fun.
Oh how I love the winter months.

Christmas is near, it's nearly come.
Fairy lights are up all around town.
Christmas trees sold from town to town.
Baubles glistening in every street window.

Yippee, it's Christmas Day.
Presents handed round and lots of early wakings.
Stockings round the fireplace bulging, almost full.
Children's happy faces getting what they asked for.

Turkey on the table ready to be eaten.
Sprouts and carrots taken from all directions.
Christmas pudding steaming, dribbled with brandy.
Drinks all round ready to be taken.

Christmas has nearly ended now.
I'll have to wait for next year.
I love those chilly winter months.
So please come again next year.

Hannah Benson (11)
St Gabriel's School, Newbury

Two Seasons

Her skin a cold white
Her hair shimmering diamonds
As it lays down on her back
The mountain snow-capped, as winter is here.

Her eyes a glittering green
With flowers in her hair
Her tears, small, sparkling ponds
Filled with water and dreams, as summer is here.

Kate Mitchell (13)
St Gabriel's School, Newbury

Little Bunny

Little bunny hop,
While he does the bunny bop.
Little bunny's tail all fluffy and white,
Carries on bopping all through the night.
He twists and turns in all his grace
And beats the tortoise in the mini sack race.

Little bunny jump
While he does the bunny bump.
Little bunny's ears all smooth and shiny,
Carry on bumping even though they're tiny.
He spins and bows in centre stage,
He's very clever for his age.

Little bunny *run*
From hunter and his gun!
Bunny's legs all blurred and fast
Are running quicker than in the past.
He dashes and dodges small as a mouse
And charges straight through the door of his house.

Catherine Armour (11)
St Gabriel's School, Newbury

I Shall Remember

Though the trees are never in bloom
And the sun is wreathed with stars
Though shadows darken the day
And does do what the raven demands.

When the night refuses the dawn
And the wolves patrol the wood
When the seasons do not obey
And the angels forget what is good.

I shall ever and always remember
The days when you were here
When all was right in the world
And the heavens were always clear.

Ailsa McCaughrean (13)
St Gabriel's School, Newbury

Miss Pussy's Disastrous Deeds

Miss Pussy, Miss Pussy, you are divine,
Miss Pussy, Miss Pussy, your black coat does shine.
Miss Pussy replied, 'You know better than that,'
Then she laughed and giggled, 'I am a cat.'

'I'm sorry I chased those pigeons,
I'm sorry I killed the rat,
I'm sorry I like to steal the milk,
All-in-all, I am a cat.'

Miss Pussy, Miss Pussy, you are divine,
Miss Pussy, Miss Pussy, your black coat does shine.
Miss Pussy replied, 'You know better than that,'
The she laughed and giggled, 'I am a cat.'

'I'm sorry, but my friends do laugh,
If I spend my whole life on the hearth,
You know I am a cuddly cat,
But life can be better if you're not so fat.'

Lucille Thompson (11)
St Gabriel's School, Newbury

The Competition

Gliding across the glimmering ice
Everyone thought I looked very nice,

My velvet dress shone so bright
Each tiny sequin catching the light,

I did a spin followed by a jump
And landed with an enormous thump,

It then dawned on me it was all over
All I had left was my four-leafed clover,

I came 3rd in the whole competition
I suppose that's a good position,

As I went home Mum told me she was so proud
And that the thump hadn't been that loud!

Kerry Gerdes-Hansen (13)
St Gabriel's School, Newbury

A Cry For Help

Why do we remember the bad times
Before we remember the good?
Why do we tease and bully
Do you really think we should?

Why do we hate some people?
We're all the same really,
The world is made for your friends,
But also for your enemies.

When someone is mean to us,
Why are we mean to them?
You can treat your friends like enemies,
But not your enemies like friends.

No one should feel sad or lonely
When going through difficult times,
You always need someone to talk to
To get it off your mind.

The world should pull together
And work as a team,
So everyone around knows
It's not as bad as it seems!

Helen Butt (11)
St Gabriel's School, Newbury

The Wind

He comes at the speed of light
So strong, knocking over his friends
He picks up an icicle and throws it at my face
I run in fear with my face burning with coldness
My tears streaming down my face
I run with all my might
But he picks me up and throws me . . .
I flee with fright.

Lily Parkinson (12)
St Gabriel's School, Newbury

In My Chocolate Box

My box is made of chocolate,
Hard and soft.

When my box is opened
The raging smell of burning cakes,
Will meet you.

The sound of the sea,
As it breezes and calms me down.

All my memories are placed in this box

Like the day I got my rabbits,
How soft the fur was.

The day when I first tasted pizza,
When the soft cheese melted in my mouth.

When I first saw a train,
A rush of excitement ran through me.

My box will last forever and ever
Filled with happy moments,
That will never leave me.

Katherine Stephens (12)
St Gabriel's School, Newbury

Night Light

Darkness is here,
Winking stars high in the sky,
The night mist, drifting in,
Frighteningly still,
The bonfire flickering,
In the distance,
A dragon's tongue, reaching out with his
Warm, hot breath.

Rebecca Irvine (13)
St Gabriel's School, Newbury

The Treasure Of Freedom

The blackness gleaming in the sun,
The softness of the fur covering the skin,
The flowing of the mane,
The boldness contained within.

The movements flow together,
He barely touches the ground,
Whilst he swiftly changes direction,
He doesn't make a sound.

He's in control and knows it,
Leader of the pack,
Until the dreadful day comes,
When he feels the first whack.

The pain sears through his body,
Confused by the strange pain,
The heavy weight on his back,
He struggles in vain.

The cold steel points dig in his side,
The metal yanking his jaw,
He's made to go and never stop,
He must not ignore.

He used to be happy,
But now he would see,
That the happiness could not come back,
He was no longer free.

Abigail Leech (14)
St Gabriel's School, Newbury

Memories

The beginning of my cruise was
like a new, squeaky balloon.
I got onto the boat and I
was absolutely amazed.
My mouth dropped open,
It was wonderful.
It looked so grand,
       so sparkly,
       so, so
       just brilliant.
Swimming every day.
Swimming in cool seawater,
then relaxing in the warm,
       bubbly Jacuzzi.
After a while of long, hard,
relaxing I got out,
to go and get ready for dinner.
But then, at the end,
I felt so sad.
It felt like all the
chocolate was gone,
the world had gone dark.
It felt like my new
balloon had . . .
    popped!

Louise Kingham (12)
St Gabriel's School, Newbury

What Shall I Write?

Should I write about dragons,
Or should I write about cats,
Maybe I could write about fairies,
Or a dirty family of rats?

I could write about marshmallows,
I could also write about you,
Should I write about homework,
Or about the number two?

I really don't know what I should write,
So maybe what I should do
Is just write about everything
And I won't forget you!

It may take me years to do,
It may only take months,
It might take a couple of days
Or maybe all my life!

Emma Darwish (11)
St Gabriel's School, Newbury

The Invisible Enemy

I run,
From an invisible enemy,
Which I cannot see, touch or smell.

I run,
From my fear and pain,
From what I regret.

I run,
Reaching towards freedom,
But I can never lose this shadow.

I run from my conscience,
A sin from the past,
A voice from the distance
Rings clear through my mind.

Clarisse Loughrey (13)
St Gabriel's School, Newbury

Black And White

Black and white
they're just colours
why do they mean
so much . . . ?

Black and white
why do we torment
and see them suffer
so much pain?

Black and white
what is the torture for?
Deep down we are all
the same.

Black and white
why should they tolerate
all this pain, for being called a
colour? It's just a name.

Sophie Kilduff (15)
St Gabriel's School, Newbury

Dreaming

A siren's song paints the waves,
Harpies fly overhead,
Flashes of light paint the sky,
A Titan there lies dead.

His back forms the mountains,
His veins a sparkling stream,
Eyes orbit high overhead,
Keeping a watch on my dreams.

Gods on Mount Olympus,
Hera there does scheme,
Hermes is the messenger,
Deliverer of dreams.

Nicola Markides (13)
St Gabriel's School, Newbury

River Flowing

The river flows ever on,
A blend of blue and green.
The river flows ever on,
Its end is never seen.

Pebbles bouncing along,
As it trickles on down,
Its ripples arranged,
Like a silvery gown.

Dancing down the mountain,
Making its own sweet way.
Through tributaries it flows,
Until it reaches the bay.

But still it sings its song,
When it rounds its final bend.
And still it sings its song,
As it reaches its very end.

Catherine Hill (13)
St Gabriel's School, Newbury

Heat

Sunlight appears.
The rays of sun stream down
On the powdery desert ground,
The fireflies are flying over the fire-heated stones,
Smoke rings rising from the ground,
The tender crimson rocks are on fire.

The blazing sun is frantically flickering,
The golden light shrivelling up the sand.
As the sun goes down, the thick warm air cools,
The sun sleeps,
Sleeps until sunrise.

Jessica Mason (13)
St Gabriel's School, Newbury

Hate

Hate is always there
Hate feeds on hate
It has the power
To destroy life itself

Hate locks people and countries
Like they are trapped
In a steel box
Deep inside they want to get out
But they can't

Hate has nearly got us all
But if we have hope
Then hate will vanish
Wars will end
Famine will not exist
The world will be better off.

Jazz O'Hagan (12)
St Gabriel's School, Newbury

Cross-Country

When I'm galloping cross-country,
I can hear his pounding feet,
Rattling the ground,
Like an earthquake beneath my feet.

The rain beating in my face,
It's feeling more like a race,
As I approach the motionless jump,
I fall and sprawl and land with a bump.

I lie there like a distilled water
droplet . . .
Soaked to the skin . . .
I can't see a thing . . .
Everything is dim . . .
He's galloping away . . .
Into the distant sunset far away . . .

Alicia Beavon (12)
St Gabriel's School, Newbury

Report On Conditions In Fairyland

Many things concern me here,
Too numerous to mention.
Below are just a few of them
To be drawn to your attention.

The children here are much neglected,
Leading a life unfettered.
Cinderella, well, she's not in school
And Tom Thumb is quite unlettered.

Thumbelina, many here believe,
Is being held hostage by the fairies.
I believe this to be a serious case,
Which really is quite scary.

The older people too are cause for worry,
For many the shops are too far.
Old Mother Hubbard is one example;
She needs access to a car.

Red Riding Hood's grandma lives alone in the wood,
She really needs re-housing.
And, on that subject, I think we need
To address the wolf's delousing.

I conclude this report with much regret,
It saddens me to say it:
'But Fairyland is a bad example
And must be eliminated.'

Jessica Welch (13)
St Gabriel's School, Newbury

Hallowe'en!

Little witches, vampires, ghosts,
We like the scary ones the most,
Run by the houses, run through the street,
Shout, 'Trick or treat!' to the people you meet,
Carving the pumpkin and putting in the lights,
So that the people coming near will get a fright!

Hiding underneath the floor,
Is a secret never to be told anymore . . .
'When all is quiet and children are tucked up in their beds,
That's when the real witches come out
And fly round the houses on their broomsticks!'

Have you seen a pointed black hat?
Does she always point out the black cat?
Does she ever say that she has been flying around all day?
This is witches work at play!

Isn't it true, when you're feeling bad,
One small hug, leaves you feeling glad!

Hiding underneath the floor,
Is a secret never to be told anymore . . .
'When all is quiet and children are tucked up in their beds,
That's when the real witches come out
And fly round the houses on their broomsticks!'

Francesca Rowley (11)
St Gabriel's School, Newbury

If I Called You A Murderer

If I called you a murderer,
Would that be too strong a word?

If I called you a friend,
Would I be telling a lie?

If I called you the enemy,
Would you fight back?

If I said I hated you,
That would be fact.

So innocent was I,
So pure and confident.
Happily accepted your praise.
You took my confidence,
You took my love
You changed me in so many ways.

What did I do to make you change?
Best friend, that's what you once called me.
Now what do you say? What do you think?
Do you even think at all?
Can you see the pain, the suffering?
Is this what you wanted all along?

If I called you a murderer,
I think you'd agree,
That all the pain inside of me,
Was caused by you and you alone.

I asked you to stop,
I ignored the remarks,
I made myself ill,
But still you persisted.

The bullying got worse,
Physical and violent,
Yet subtle, no one noticed a thing.
I cut, cut deep down, it satisfied me,
I could control it.
Unlike the pain inside my head, ongoing, never-ending.

I'm left without a soul, heart and feelings.
You've left me numb, lifeless.
Just a shell wasting away.

I was once like you,
Full of life, love and happiness.
A bright flame burning constantly.
Now knowing, I should have spoken out,
Told someone, a friend.
But it's too late now.

If I called you a murderer,
Would that be too strong a word?

Louise Sheridan (14)
St Gabriel's School, Newbury

The Wind, Friend Or Enemy?

The wind is shouting at the rustling leaves
Waiting for an answer silent, silent

Gradually building up to an angry howl
Like a werewolf in the glistening moon

It broadcasts its news
To people far and wide

Not giving a care
About thinking out aloud

It becomes quiet or loud
Depending on how it feels

Blowing, howling
Shouting for no reason

It has to learn to be more silent
Also to be more forgiving

Friend to only the seed
From which we get new life

Then it suddenly dies
Because of the sun.

Katy Pasternakiewicz (13)
St Gabriel's School, Newbury

Walk Into The Outback

There's a creepy atmosphere,
A moonless sky,
Not a murmur, a whisper,
Or a stir of bush life.
A rush of cold wind,
seems to angrily howl,
While the merciless animals,
Begin their dawning prowl.
In my fear I fidget
And shuffle slowly down,
My eyes suddenly widen,
With my constant deepening frown.
I hear a faint echo
And I wish I were at home,
The rippling water
Travels over worn stones.
Faint mating howls of dingoes,
Flip-flap-flip of leathery wings,
Belonging to bats or flying foxes,
The owl's tune joyfully sings.
A lumbering wombat fed,
It shambled near, unfettered,
As I looked, I quivered and fled.
The hoot of a mopoke,
Fills an empty sky,
I am lost in my dreams,
With a steady sunrise.

Lara Woodhead (13)
St Gabriel's School, Newbury

Inner Beauty

A head so round and bright,
A face full of colour and light,
The stem, the body a rich shade of green,
Supporting its weight with a stem so lean.

These flowers of mine sit on my table,
The little one is small, but still perfectly able
To grow as big as the rest,
To stand in his vase and look his best.

For size doesn't matter,
You could be thinner or fatter,
As long as what's inside is good;
You must try to be nice and act as you should.

My mother did tell me what I should do,
But I now pass the message right down to you,
You mustn't judge a person by the colour of their skin,
What's most important is what's hidden within.

Charlotte Bowen (13)
St Gabriel's School, Newbury

Awaken Night

Great, dark, dilapidated tunnel
Unknown hoot
Slowly creeping cat
Eyes flickery
Rippling, slipping dew
Dedicated dingo shambled by the moonless sky
Clown-like kookaburra grins
Flying foxes in deep slumber
A wombat awakes to escape the sun horizon
Snakes follow the scent of the nearest pool
As the sun slowly awakes from its midnight wander
The magic of the night creeps away
Only leaving day, now to play.

Nicola London (13)
St Gabriel's School, Newbury

The Solar System

Millions and millions of miles away,
Is a location quite different from ours.
And let me say, that this place far away,
Includes a planet called Mars.
It's red and it's hot and it's made out of rock.
There are sightings of some kind of life.
While Jupiter's vast and it spins around so fast,
That storms happen all day and night.
Saturn's here next, although you might feel perplexed,
That its rings are visible from Earth.
Uranus and Neptune are next in the line
They are similar size and girth.
Pluto so small, is the furthest of all
It's as frozen as frozen can be.
Back here on Earth, is where life was first
Earth's covered with land and sea.
Getting nearer the sun,
Is Venus the one with no water, but volcanoes there?
Mercury's craters were formed when asteroids swarmed.
Too hot here for settlers to even dare
The star of them all with its burning-hot wall,
Shoots out rays of warmth and light.
Some planets you'll find out soon, have a number of moons,
That act as a satellite.
The galaxy is the nine planets we see,
Including billions of stars.
This phenomenal sight is special all right,
We are even amazed from afar!

Chelsie Paul (12)
St Gabriel's School, Newbury

The Society On The Moon

In the society on the moon,
The inhabitants are green, red and blue.
They have no name,
They do not age,
They do not laugh or rage.
The mayor here, who's not too bright
And is easily tricked and fooled,
Was persuaded one day
Without much effort be afraid
To introduce food colouring into food.
The people turned purple
And yellow and pink
And a shade of strange indigo.
It was founded one day,
That if a pink breeds with a purple
And the blue breeds pink,
A strange new colour would evolve.
This colour was odd and indescribable,
If you stared at it long you may faint,
It was a bright as white, yet as dull as black
And as deep as the ocean wide,
It caused much confusion
And so in conclusion,
The inhabitants of the moon all died.
The moral of this story,
I'm sure you will realise,
Is, if you are the mayor of the moon inhabitants
Don't be fooled by a liar's lies.

Alice Stirmey (13)
St Gabriel's School, Newbury

My Box

My box is made of wind and air,
Rippling through my hair.
Inside my box I would place,
The high and breezy cliffs,
Towering above a smooth and sandy beach.
The gentle water lapping at the shore, quiet and tranquil
Or maybe stormy, dark and angry,
Roaring like an enormous lion.

And in my box I would also place,
A tall and winding tree,
A laurel tree which I used to climb
And stare up at the stars.
Lying in my leafy bed
The cold air biting at my face.
The sense of freedom, no fears, no troubles
Escaping into imagination.

The splash of water, deep blue water
Cold and refreshing
Never-ending happiness,
The crunch of soft, white snow,
Beneath my feet,
The first feet to walk there.
The rush of air, the sound of the wheels beneath my feet,
as the board flies down an empty road.
All these things and more I would place in my box, my life.

Natasha Turner (13)
St Gabriel's School, Newbury

The Cat

Crouching low,
Every muscle tensed,
As his fierce yellow eyes
Stare with a fixed intensity.
How can his prey resist
His hypnotic presence?

A rustle of movement in the grass
And in response he can't resist
An anticipatory twitch of the tail,
Lowering onto his haunches before
Lunging forward with all of his might
And in a second it's over,
With a satisfied lick of a paw.

In the heat of the day,
All seems sleepy,
Even the flies drone slowly by.
On the wall my cat lifts his head,
Drugged by the noonday sun,
Happily absorbing heat
Through his outstretched body.

By the fire he now lies sleeping,
Carelessly extending
A black leg forward.
A twitch of an ear to check all is well,
Before curling his tail
Back under his chin.

Claire Nicoll (12)
St Gabriel's School, Newbury

Things That Make Me Glad

My box emerges from the white clouds,
Like sunbeams bursting forth at dawn,
Lighting up my day.
Happiness locked within,
Memories of joyful times
Spent with family and friends.
The smell of freshly baked bread,
Filling the winter air.
The crunch of snow as I place my feet
In the clean, white powder.
The hot, spicy aroma of Indian meals,
Poppadoms exploding in sizzling oil.
At the beach, the white horses breaking at my feet.
The warm, white sand and the cool, clean sea.
The towering cliffs, the seagulls wheeling overhead.
The salty sea air, dogs splashing in the water,
Children building castles, having fun.
The spirit of a team, working together,
As one fluid movement, scoring a goal.
The things that make me glad
I keep safe in this box, so I will never lose them.

Helen Brandwood (13)
St Gabriel's School, Newbury

My Box Of Memories

My box is made of happy times,
all the precious things to me.
Lasting memories, thoughts and smells,
Things I've done and seen.

Walking on the shore,
water lapping at my feet.
Snowflakes falling,
drifting to the sheets of snow.

Watching my sister,
dance gracefully on the stage.
Jumping down the stairs,
anticipating Christmas morning.

The smell of bacon,
sizzling and spitting in the pan.
The trickle of water,
running down a stream.

My box is made of happy times,
all the precious things to me.
Lasting memories, thoughts and smells,
things I've done and seen.

Charlotte Keast (12)
St Gabriel's School, Newbury

What Is Love?

You cannot see it
But you know that it's there;
Love
You can feel it all around
As it wanders through the air;
Love.

As it grows in you,
So you grow with one another;
Love.
It touches your heart
Like a gentle breeze in the summer;
Love.

A kind, caring word
Can make someone's day;
Love.
It directs you in the dark,
So you can go the right way;
Love.

Love is gentle and amiable
To the sick, deaf and blind.
It is not rude and doesn't anger;
Love is patient and kind.

Emma Constantine (14)
St Gabriel's School, Newbury

Impressions

The eye of the human,
With its brilliant colours.
The powder on the lids;
Give an impression.

The clothes of the human,
Bright, dull, flowery, plain.
Long, short, holey, full;
Give an impression.

The size of the human,
Small, large, fat, thin.
Flat stomach or rounded;
Gives an impression.

All the features of a human
Give an impression.
Whether they are beautiful or ugly;
We always judge people on their appearances.

Becky Brown (13)
St Gabriel's School, Newbury

My Sister!

My sister is one you wouldn't forget,
My sister is one that is very bad,
My sister is one that hides things,
My sister is one that drives you mad,
My sister is one that runs off with your shoes,
My sister is one that is awfully crafty,
My sister is one that hits you hard,
My sister is one that draws on your homework,
My sister is one that eats your lunch,
My sister is one that won't hold your hand,
My sister is one that doesn't have a bath,
My sister is one that moans all the time
But sometimes she can be the slightest bit good!

Bridie Green (12)
Sandhurst School

Sad Thoughts

(In loving memory of Liam Mintern)

I arrive home from school to my mum and dad
One look at their faces they looked so sad
The news they told me cut so deep
My cousin Liam had died in his sleep.

A seizure they say, no one to blame
It took him so quickly with no suffering or pain
Eleven years old so much life left to live
His jokes, his smiles, so much love did he give.

Christmases and birthdays such fun that we had
Dressed as a girl, he looked raving mad
I think of the fun times and remember his voice
Why would God do this, is it through choice?

Eighteen months have now passed, but it feels like yesterday
Will these feelings of sadness, guilt and hurt ever go away?
Weekends at my grandparents are so different for me
I have lost my best friend and now the four of us are only three.

I look at his mum with her sad, hollow face
Does she think about God, does she ever say grace?
His young brother playing, but he still remembers
Because he lost his mate, such a close family member.

A holiday was booked to Florida we were to go
But with Liam's death it was not to be so
Now I am going, his photo I will take
I will go on scary rides just for his sake.

As I get older his memory will stay strong
And I know I will realise that I've done nothing wrong
His mum, dad and brother will never replace
Their handsome, strong son with his lovely smiling face.

Kirsty Currier (13)
Sandhurst School

A Delightful Day!

In the distance, the mist is swirling,
The grey-blue clouds curling,
Daylight is beginning to break,
The water is like a mystifying long lake,
The blue floating sky above,
Is what I love.

The waves crashing onto the beach,
Then rolling back just out of reach,
The tidy, craggy rockpools,
Which the crabs use for their tools,
The children's laughter as they play,
But what do you say? Hooray!

The birds are singing early in the morning,
As the new day is dawning,
The squiggly, wiggly worms glide along,
Waiting for the right song,
The crunching underfoot of the leaves,
Reminds you of that distant sea.

As the crystal clear icicles begin to melt,
It is what the day has dealt,
The sun begins to set on the horizon,
As my mind begins to wisen,
The red-gold glow in the meadow,
Casts its early evening glow on the hedgerow.

Pitch dark black the sky is now,
The stars are saying: 'Wow!'
Tu-whit, tu-whoo, tu-whit, tu-whoo go the owls of the night,
As the birds get ready for their flight,
The moon is saying, 'Goodnight,
I hope you sleep tight.'

Emma Glover (12)
Sandhurst School

Entwined Ballad

The stars were shining
in the dark, moonlit sky.
He was short of timing
so he began to cry.

The trees rustled in the breeze,
his gloves fell out of his pocket,
they were followed by the keys,
then he found a locket.

I felt the ring in my jacket
and I started to shake,
would I be able to hack it?
I hope she's not a fake.

I saw her standing there
while holding my diamond ring,
a little worse for wear!
Is this the real thing?

Rebecca Taylor (13)
Sandhurst School

What If?

What if you never die?
What if the sea overflowed?
What if you could change the world?
What if we had no Queen or parliament?
What if I could go into the future?
What if I had never turned that corner?
What if there was no school?
What if you never grew up?
What if monsters were real?
What if films could come true?
What if there were no such words as 'what if'?

Helen Dewsnap (13)
Sandhurst School

Entwined Ballad

The stars were shining
In the dark, moonlit sky.
He was short of timing
So he began to cry.

The trees rustled in the breeze,
His gloves fell out of his pocket,
They were followed by the keys,
Then he found a locket.

The stars were dancing,
Far, far up above,
The trees were prancing,
As she found a glove.

As she searched her pocket,
She couldn't find a thing,
Where was her locket
And her diamond ring?

I felt the ring in my jacket
And I started to shake,
Would I be able to hack it,
I hope she's not a fake?

He said he'd meet me here,
Was he just a fake?
This is my worst fear,
I'm starting to shake.

I saw her standing there
While holding my diamond ring,
A little worse for wear!
Is this the real thing?

I see him standing there,
Holding my diamond ring,
A little worse for wear,
Is this the real thing?

Chloe Soane (14) & Rebecca Taylor (13)
Sandhurst School

Trainers

I've seen this pair of trainers
The ones I really want
The label's right
The colour's right
They're just right for my foot.

There's a problem with these trainers
The ones I really want
The design is right
The pattern's right
The price of course is not.

I begged my mum to buy them
The ones I really like
The label's right
The colour's right
My mum said, 'On your bike!'

Oliver Lammas (13)
Sandhurst School

Sweet Lil' Fish

Fishing is such a great pleasure,
Catching a big one is like a treasure.

It's so peaceful and so quiet,
Getting away from all the riot.

It could be big, it could be small,
That's just the fun of it all.

You could catch trout, you could catch salmon,
Please don't eat them, just eat gammon.

You could do coarse, you could play a match,
Look in my keep net, what did I catch?

Please don't kill them, don't eat them for tea,
Just let them swim in the deep blue sea!

Jody Lees (13)
Sandhurst School

What If . . . ?

What if I hadn't turned that corner?
I wouldn't have seen that terrible sight,
What if, what if I hadn't looked back
I wouldn't be standing here with fear and fright,
All alone in the dark, smelly alley,
I stood and watched the moon go by.
Soon after it had vanished, it got very late,
Then my phone rang, it must have been fate!
At that time I was petrified with shivers running down my spine,
Then I realised who it was on my phone,
It turned out to be my best friend, Joan.
She wanted to know if I could go for tea?
I couldn't answer as I saw the figure lying before me.
I got closer and closer,
I couldn't hear a sound,
My heart was pounding,
No answer was to be found,
I bent down and stroked her face,
She looked so pale, yet full of grace,
She had no pulse and no heart beating,
What if, what if I hadn't turned that corner?

Siân Ledlie (12)
Sandhurst School

My Grandad!

My grandad drives a taxi all day,
That has always been his way,
He drives in London all day long
And always sings a happy song,
When I go to visit him
He give me sweets, crisps and drink,
I love my grandad very much,
I ring him lots to keep in touch.

Lauren Fitts (12)
Sandhurst School

Love And Hate

I love you, I love you, I hate you,
I hate you, I love you, I don't.
I want you - I just want to hate you
I just want to love you, but won't.

You make me unhappy, I hate you,
I loathe you and that is a fact,
Get out of my life or I'll kill you,
Hey, where are you going? Come back!

Don't leave me, I love you, I loathe you.
You're brutal, you're charming, you're me.
You're my one and only, I love you,
Get out of my life or I'll scream!

I love you, you're special, you're nothing
You've no one, you're someone quite dear,
I hate you, I miss you, I love you,
I hope that I've made myself clear.

Sukhdeep Sond (12)
Sandhurst School

What If?

What if the life we lead is in the pathway of trouble?
What if there was no life and we are merely dreams?
What if life is a hint of what we believe in?
What if dreams were true, where would we be standing?
What if there was no life after death and we cease to be?
What if the future we are to live has been meddled with?
What if I am a phantom, a ghost and I never existed?
What if things we see are illusions, which we treat real?
What if the world we live in was never there?
What if I had known the dangers that lurked in the shadows?
What if the life I lead is meaningless and I am wasting my time?
What if death is when I surface from a finished dream?
What if the people we think we know are strangers?
What if each time I sleep, it is hibernation?

Shanti Rai (12)
Sandhurst School

Holiday

My holiday in the sun is near,
It's the time I most look forward to,
The coolest waves and the hottest sun,
I'm hoping to have lots of fun.

We check in to the hotel room,
Choose our beds and unpack the cases,
We head downstairs and look around,
I think this is the best we've found.

The days are spent on the sandy beach,
Riding pedaloes and water skiing,
When the sun just gets too much
And the sun is just too hot to touch,
We head under the coolest shade
And hope our suntan doesn't fade.

The night times are when the party begins,
Lots to eat and liquors to drink,
Karaoke and casinos to play,
I hope to have a go as a beginner and come out on top as a winner,
The discos are well on the way,
This surely is the best part of the day.

Carl Farrell (12)
Sandhurst School

Untitled

I wandered slowly through the sea,
Trying to find a friend for me,
Searching around high and low,
I couldn't think where else to go,
Then one day I spied a cray,
Now I have a friend, hooray!

Zoe Green (12)
Sandhurst School

Alphabet Poem

A ngelica, the angry ant, ate apples and amber apricots all day.
B illy bought big baked beans for a big breakfast.
C hristopher carried some carrots in a container.
D igging dangerously, the dog dumps the dynamite.
E ventually Emma enters the room.
F rogs from France, feed on flies.
G irls giggle, gossiping about their granny.
H arry hid Holly's hideous face.
 I n India, Ian interrupts the interpreter.
J umping with joy, Jimmy jogs.
K aren cries, carrying the kettle.
L abelling the lighted lantern, Lilly lies on her lunch.
M ia munches on mushrooms in the museum.
N obody knows Noddy at nightfall.
O val orchids stand out.
P eople play politely in the pool.
Q ueens quarters quibble quietly.
R ushing round, Rohan's writing one word.
S uzie sat down, staring at the sun in the sky.
T easing Tom, the teacher teaches the team table tennis.
U nder the umbrella, Uri understands.
V iolins and violets are vividly clear.
W illiam wonders what to do.
'X cellent cat carries exciting and extraordinary videos.
Y ellow yo-yos yonder.
Z igzagging zip zooms all the way down to the zoo to see the zebras.

Emma Swinyard (12)
Sandhurst School

What If . . . ?

What if the world was flat?
Like a blue gym mat
What if we fell on God's head like a cap?
Fell onto his map
Then onto his lap
And then onto a very large mousetrap?

What if we had no law?
All the robbers would want more.
What if they took out a giant claw
Which they used as a big saw
And made all people sore?

What if there was no school?
Everyone would think it was cool
They would be out in the pool
Or playing pool
All the teachers say, 'Oh dear.'
All because they lost their career.

What if we had no friends?
It is something you can never mend
They will never lend
Money or even spend.
Everyone would be there to offend
I don't think I would like that in the end.

What if there was no world?
After all it is very old
But God would be told
Not to let it crease or fold.
Or you never know it might start to mould,
But what if all this was true?

David Fallows (12)
Sandhurst School

Megan

She greets me every morning
Wagging her long, fluffy tail
She looks at me with her big brown eyes
Hoping I'm going to play.

We like to walk together
She likes to chase big sticks
She loves to swim in the water
Best of all she likes to lick
She doesn't like loud noises
She's frightened of the dark
She doesn't like cats
They always make her bark.

She's a big part of the family
We love her all the time
I say she was my best friend
I'm very glad she's mine.

Daniel Ball (12)
Sandhurst School

A Bouncy Ball

A bouncy ball bouncing around
Breaking cups
Shattering glass
Bouncing up the stairs
Then bouncing down again
Bouncing off the walls
Bouncing off the lights
Bouncing out the window
Bouncing off the kerb
Hitting the cars
Hitting the bikes
Over the fence
Over the tree
Into the pot
Then down the drain.

Kieren Charman (12)
Sandhurst School

My Secret Hideaway!

Beyond the wood it lay,
Its secrets safe with me.
A secret hideaway,
A lovely place to be.

A pretty pink petal,
The buzz of a bee,
A harmful stinging nettle,
It's all special to me.

The shadow of the tree,
The sun shines bright,
Birds singing with glee,
Gone quiet at night.

The twinkle of stars,
Like soft fairy lights,
A hoot of an owl,
The sounds of the night.

The sun comes out to play,
Sleepy animals awake,
It's the start of a new day,
In my secret hideaway!

Lorna Glazier (13)
Sandhurst School

Grandma

Grandma, why did you have to leave
And make us come to grieve?
Oh Grandma we miss you so!
Grandma, why does Grandad cry,
and always say your name?
Oh Grandma we miss you so!
Grandma, why did you have to go?
You knew we loved you so!

Samantha Adlington (12)
Sandhurst School

The Strip

The lights blinded out the darkness,
as I first set foot on the strip.
But amazing as it seemed,
seven days lay ahead and perhaps, a championship.

I'd never been to a place like Vegas,
I'd never seen so many lights like this before.
Lights burning through the night, in this town that never slept,
where all arrive in credit, but most depart in debt.

I walked on down the street,
passed a thousand open doors.
Where a million slot machines spew,
their contents to electric floors.

Static flies through the air,
my every nerve's alive.
Seven days, how many fights,
was I sure I could survive?

It came to the day of the main event,
I woke up feeling tired and tense.
I made it through to the final round,
I had it good and then pound, pound, pound.

His blows flew from left to right,
in the end I lost the fight.
I walked back to my team feeling down,
they all smiled, whilst I just frowned.

They knew I'd won a medal,
but I hadn't yet worked that out.
Then they called my name,
boy you should have heard me shout.

My dream trip ended, I said goodbye,
My week had flown, in the blink of an eye.

Jacob Addley-Pickford (12)
Sandhurst School

Shadow Man

When you're outside on Hallowe'en
And you hear footsteps close by
The clackety-clack of a horse running
And a humming soft and dry.

Once you hear those awful sounds
That's the time to run
But if you stay there, standing still
The Shadow Man will come.

His horse is black like the dark, dark night
And he wears a big black cape
And once his humming slows right down
There's definitely no escape.

He stops his horse quite near you
And jumps quickly to the ground
Then starts to walk towards you
Without making a single sound.

The tension grows much stronger
As he pulls out a sharp knife
He cuts and bruises and stabs at you
As you run for your life.

You run for what seems like hours,
Until you finally run out of breath
But the Shadow Man has disappeared
And now there's nothing left.

But although you think he's dead and gone
The Shadow Man still lives on.
His horse will still clack, clack, clack
And the Shadow Man will be back.

Rebekah McVittie (13)
Sandhurst School

The Shopping Spree!

S hop till you drop,
H urts your feet, but you just can't stop,
O verall your feet are sore, but you are,
P leased as you can't carry anymore!
P leasing to know that your card can't take any more bashing!
I n approved smile you buy your last item,
N o way has 6 hours
G one all ready.

T he time is up, the shops are shutting,
I ndeed, your shopping spree has come to an end, but hey, I
L ove shopping,
L oving shopping is a part of me.

Y ou broke the bank, but hey!
O ut come the old clothes and in come the new!
U are beginning to feel a bit sad as you leave the car park,
                                but just remember that you're
R eady for more shopping, tomorrow!

F eet are hurting and your legs ache,
E nd of the day,
E nd of your shopping spree,
T he day is not over yet, till you have paraded around your
                                living room.

H urrying all the bags away,
U are in debt and your purse is flowing with receipts, you
R a live wire and you're going partying tonight to show off
                                your new outfits, go you!
T he moral of this poem is *shop till your feet hurt!*

Chloé Osborne (12)
Sandhurst School

What If?

What if I turn the corner,
And a lion jumped out at me,
A mouse, a rat or even a dog or a cat?
I don't know what I would see.
What if, what if, what if?

What if tomorrow never comes,
I won't see my best friend, Mum, Dad or even my school ever again.
I won't be able to watch telly or even fill my belly.
I won't hear the pattering of the rain, although it drives me insane,
What if, what if, what if?

What if I hadn't have known?
Known what?
Known that the sweet shop was shut.
Known that the sun was so hot.
What if, what if, what if?

What if the world ends?
What will happen? Where will I go? What will I do?
Maybe the world will start again, I don't know
And what about the kangaroos in the zoos.
What if, what if, what if?

What if my family died?
I would have no one, no one at all.
Maybe my nan or granddad or even gran.
What would I do? Who would I call?
What if, what if, what if?

What if there was no sun?
We would all die, wouldn't we?
I wouldn't be able to see anyone ever again.
What would happen to all the bumblebees?
What if, what if, what if?

Gina Gardner (12)
Sandhurst School

Pets

Pets are fun, pets are great,
They're really as good as your best mate.

Pets need love, pets need a home,
Often pets need a really good comb.

Pets need exercise, pets need food,
If they don't they'll be in a mood.

If pets are sick, if pets are ill,
The vet will help I'm sure he will.

Pets need company, pets want cuddles,
When they're young they make a lot of puddles.

Pets need care, pets need water,
Some of them have a son or daughter.

Over all it's really hard work, but you think it's great,
As they're still your best mate!

Emma Hood (12)
Sandhurst School

It's A Secret?

Smash, splash, crash, bash go the waves of the sea.
I never thought this day would come, when they would start to flee.
They jump so high and full of grace,
Their echo sounds you'll have to brace.
Their rubber skin that is so smooth,
Their pointed fins that help them move.
Every morning wake up at seven,
Smell the air it's just like Heaven.
In my bathing suit ran to the shore,
I have to swim up to the moor.
The best view's there, I say it is,
They jump so fast, *whizz, whizz, whizz.*
The deep blue sea that they live in,
Yes you're right it's the dolphins.

Becky Bird (13)
Sandhurst School

The Old Woman

In an old, cosy café, my mum and me,
Sat munching our buns and drinking our tea.
All were fine and the sun shone bright
The café was a picture, a wonderful sight.

But in stepped a woman with scruffy old hair,
Plump and round with skin so fair.
People stared at her old wrinkly face
They shook their heads and said, 'What a disgrace!'

Then all of a sudden, she bowed her head down,
The smiles on her face then turned to a frown.
She rose to her feet and picked up a chair,
She tore it apart as if she didn't care.

Other people did nothing, they simply looked away
They turned their backs and said, 'Just go away!'
The old woman then burst into tears,
She left the old café to shouting and jeers.

The lady ran off, as quick as could be
While the people in the café sat drinking their tea.
They all just sat there, nobody asked
Why the old woman was acting daft.

No one tried to help, they all stood scared
No one would talk to her, nobody dared.
They all just thought, *oh, she looks weird!*
So they whispered and bickered and giggled and sneered.

And to the people in the café I want you to know,
She got that treatment wherever she'd go.
It hurt her so much that she cried and cried
And a week later, she committed suicide.

Sam Oakford (13)
Sandhurst School

Columbia Shuttle Disaster

The astronauts went through their pre-flight checks,
To make sure there couldn't be any defects.

The checks were complete and countdown on,
A little time after the shuttle had gone.

The shuttle was away within a second,
All the astronauts saw the gates of space beckon.

All the crew began their on-board work,
Anyone who didn't was considered a jerk.

The space shuttle veered right,
Space was as dark and cold as a mid-winter's night.

After a month their long mission ended,
When the space station wing became mended.

Once again they went through the pre-flight checks,
Just to make sure there couldn't be any defects.

The checks were complete and countdown on,
A short time after the shuttle was gone.

The shuttle screamed down towards Earth,
From the cockpit you could see the city of Perth.

As the shuttle began its final decent,
The view from the shuttle was very pleasant.

The anxious onlookers cringe,
As the shuttle starts to singe.

In a raging ball of fire the shuttle combusts,
And rains down on Texas as a cloud of dust.

The onlookers cry in despair,
This kind of disaster is so very rare.

William Savage (13)
Sandhurst School

The Ghost Child

I dread the darkness coming
I wish the sun would stay
For she comes alive at night
And silently sleeps through the day

She carefully creeps through the door
And gently whispers my name
She pleads to play with me
She pleads to play a game

Illuminating the darkness
She solemnly sits on my bed
I don't know if she's alive
Or if she's really dead

Her face makes my heart skip a beat
So pale, lifeless and thin
Shadowed rings around her eyes
Moulding, murky skin

Her clothes are ragged and torn
Her shoes are caked in mud
Her legs are bruised and dry
Her mouth is dripping blood

She wants to be my friend
But timidly I say no
She screams at me with rage
And thankfully turns to go

She comes here every night
She sneaks into my room
My eyes are welling with tears
For I know she'll come back soon.

Sophie Coster (13)
Sandhurst School

My Poem

This is my poem,
Please read it.
It's not about you, it's not about me.
It's about a dog and a cat actually.
This is their poem of love . . .

They met in a car,
While the dog was eating a Mars bar
And the cat purred,
'Let me have some please!'

So both of them sat on top of the car.
Both dog and the cat sharing the Mars bar,
Looked up at the stars and sighed,
'I'm so far from home and I've just missed the last flight.
Oh what am I going to do?'

'Where do you live?' both of them asked.
'In California!' both replied.
'Me too!' both dog and cat shouted out aloud,
Then both sighed again and looked up at the clouds.

The cat said, 'My mum, my dad and my sisters three,
I wonder if they're missing me?'
The dog said, 'I'm sure they are.
If it was me, I wouldn't have even let you go this far!'
The cat looked at the dog and blushed.

They both sat in silence for a very long time,
Till the dog shouted out, 'Since we're both going to California,
Why don't we both go in my car?
It's got plenty of fuel to last us for days.
So tell me, what do you say?'

The cat cried out, 'Oh my, I'm not quite sure.
This is really too sudden, you know!'
'Oh come on!' the dog said. 'It will be fun,
Soon we'll be in California and I'll be gone!'

'Okay!' the cat shouted out.
'Okay!' the dog agreed
So both of them went in the car,
Which had lots of fuel to take them very far.

They soon reached California,
Both said their goodbyes and left each other
But met up the next day and the next,
And soon lived happily ever after.

Dina Rai (13)
Sandhurst School

A Day In The Life Of School

Beep beep, goes your alarm clock in the morning,
Time for school, but it's all so boring.
You drag your body to get a shower,
Can't I go back to sleep for one more hour?
You force your body downstairs and eat,
Next get changed, nice and neat.
Pack your bag ready for school,
Bring the right books and don't look like a fool.
You arrive at school and feel very sad,
As every single lesson is 100% bad.
Time is slugging by,
I think I'd rather die!
Science, maths, French and history, followed by lunch,
A time to eat my food munch by munch.
A time to relax but not so fast!
You've got dreadful geography last.
You keep your eyes fixed on the clock,
Paying no attention, but *tick-tock, tick-tock.*
The bell finally rings and you're out of here,
Within five minutes this place will be clear.
You walk home with your friends, can't wait to get home,
You're free from this place, free to roam.
You get home and ring the doorbell,
Thinking of tomorrow, the next dosage of Hell.

Marcus Hau (13)
Sandhurst School

What Is Heaven?

What is Heaven?
Is it all clouds and candy?

Will I be there for eternity?
Or can I visit Earth?

Will I see angels?
Flying all around?

Will I see God?
The powerful Almighty?

The people who have died,
Will they look the same?

What is Heaven?
Is it all clouds and candy?

Bianca Davanzo (12)
Sandhurst School

The Dead Of Night

In the dead of night
In the midnight black
You get a fright
Nice feelings you lack.

Something creeps up
You jump with fear
You grab your cup
And take a sip of your beer.

You start to calm down
You start to relax
You put on your gown
Your fear hits the max!

Danielle Utton (13)
Sandhurst School

Memories!

I wish they wouldn't argue,
They start shouting loud.
The neighbours always seem to talk,
About my parents and their rows.

When they start shouting,
I go up to my room.
I sit there crying
And hope it stops soon.

You hear the glasses smashing,
And the bang of a fist,
My mum will start weeping,
I hope my dad has missed.

He would storm out the house,
And to the pub I guess.
My mum would moan and groan,
And start to clear up the mess.

At least they are divorced now,
And my mum doesn't get bruised
But I still have the memories,
Which I will never lose.

Elise Crayton (13)
Sandhurst School

Death

D eath is something not to fear,
E ven to shed a weary tear,
A ll good things must come to an end,
T he lives of all eventually descend
H is or hers fears escalating into devilish nightmares.

Matthew Hegarty (13)
Sandhurst School

The Four Seasons

In spring it's the start of a new year;
The flowers start to come out.
We might get some sun, we might get some rain;
That's not all that spring's about.

The spring leads into the summer,
Supposedly the best and hottest season of all.
We're all found in T-shirts and shorts;
Yet we still can't get cool.

Autumn is coming upon us,
Leaves are falling off the trees;
They are turning all different colours,
It is quite pleasing to see.

Finally we have winter,
We all moan that we are cold.
We might make snowmen and have snowball fights.
I think winter's the most fun season of all.

Alex Oliver (13)
Sandhurst School

Candles

They come in all shapes
Square, circle, heart and star.
They come in all sizes
Small, medium and large.
They come in all colours
Blue, red, yellow, pink and green.
It helps you see in the dark
When the lights are gone.
All is not lost
As the candle gives you light.
At night any time, anywhere
The candle will help.

Jessica Anderson (13)
Sandhurst School

A Boy Named Theo

There was a boy named Theo,
His parents didn't care.
They made him do all the household chores,
He had nothing clean to wear.

While he did all the housework,
His parents loitered by the pool.
While his mum and dad ate lobster,
He was forced to live off gruel.

School wasn't much better,
He was bullied by all the other kids.
He was beaten up with hockey sticks,
And hit with dustbin lids.

He always got detention,
As his homework was never in on time.
This was because his parents,
Made him clear up their dirt and grime.

One day he just lost it,
He ran straight out of school.
His parents didn't notice, he ran past their house
As they were relaxing by the pool.

Theo ran for miles and miles,
He ran down lane after lane.
And at the first chance he got,
He threw himself under a speeding train.

His parents didn't care he was dead,
They just adopted another one.
They made little Thomas do all the work,
That Theo had once done.

I feel sorry for young Thomas,
He may never live like you and me.
He might never know just how grand,
This world we live in can be.

Jack Hicks (13)
Sandhurst School

Dancing

The teacher says, 'Point those toes!
Now straighten your back!
Tummies in, chest out!
Now stretch your arms!'
All at the same time
What does she think I am?
I thought this was supposed to be fun
Now to the bar
But not for a drink
She shows us what to do
You must be joking, I think
She stands behind me
And waits for my move.
'I can do it,' I say to myself.
Positive thinking must help.
I stand on the tips of my toes.
'Hold for 10,' she yells.
The pain, I think.
The bell rings, lesson over.
Thank God, I think.
'Same time next week!'
'Yippee!' we all squeal.
Why, oh why, oh why, didn't I take up football?

Samantha Dick (13)
Sandhurst School

Friends

F riends are important,
R eally important they are.
I play football with my friends.
E very friend I have
N ever lets me down.
D efinitely I need my friends.
S urely friends are important?

Adam James (13)
Sandhurst School

The Leptictidium

L eaping through the woodland
E scaping open jaws
P icking up the smallest bugs
T ackling them with her claws
I nside her small nest
C rouching very low
T his bundle of nervous energy
I s cat-like in size
D angerous carnivores around her
I t is hard to survive, but never
U nderestimate what a leptictidium knows
M oved on has this creature, so no one really knows!

Hayley Thair (14)
Sandhurst School

The Day Until

'Do you want to come out and play?'
'Sorry I can't come out today.
I think I have a cold, I must be ill,
I'm quite warm but I have a chill.'
I went to the doctor, he looked and said,
'You'll need a few days in bed.'
After a day or two in bed she came and said,
'You look a bit better, you're not so red.
I think you can go out today,
Just wrap up warm when you go and play!'

Kelly Daniels (12)
Sandhurst School

Smartie!

I have a four-legged cat,
She likes to sit on my lap.
When she crunches her food,
You know she's getting in a mood.
She loves to play,
Most of the time we play all day.
She attacks my feet,
And then turns very sweet.
She doesn't like other cats,
But loves to chase the rats.
She's cute, cuddly and fluffy,
I love my cat,
She's great.

Sarah Charter (13)
Sandhurst School

My Wish

I have a wish I want to tell,
If we have time before the bell.
I want to tell about the wish,
It is as simple as a swish -
A swish of leaves, stiff on the ground,
A swish of wind without a sound.
Nobody knows what my wish is,
My mind is full of things like this.
I wish our world was full of peace,
My wish is simple just like this!

Ann Ovcharenko (13)
Sandhurst School

Forest

Galloping through the forest,
sun shining through the trees.
Everything was peaceful,
and made me feel at ease.

If I were to reach my destination,
I would have to ride all day.
By night we'd be so tired,
we couldn't wait to hit the hay.

I knocked on the door,
is there someone there, anyone at all?
I heard a noise, stood poised,
to see only a lonely owl.

I decided to go, as it started to snow,
and didn't want to get stuck.
So I struck up my horse,
and galloped away into the night.

Leigh-Michael Anderson (13)
The Oratory School

Skill And Clumsiness

I am skill
I am the free kick curled round the wall
The amazing run down the wing
The perfectly played tune
The expertly painted picture
I am skill

I am clumsiness
I am the banged head
The untied shoelace
The dropped lunch
The spilt paint
I am clumsiness.

Bertie Baker-Smith (12)
The Oratory School

My Shark

In the park one morning,
Watching shapes in the pool,
A monstrous fish was yawning,
And then began to drool.

Watched it for a while,
And realised it was stranded,
I would have run a mile,
But I did not understand it.

I took it home in a bag,
And put it in my pond,
Its flippers started to sag,
But I grew kind of fond.

I fed it pond weed and a pie,
Another fish as well,
He got kind of high,
And downwardly he fell!

I did not want him anymore,
So I rang London Zoo
The man he would not come for him,
So I flushed him down the loo.

Aidan Keeble (13)
The Oratory School

Bravery

I am the key skill for an army,
I shine through the ranks,
Filling their hearts with power.
I am what makes the people
Stand up for themselves against tyranny.
I am the downfall of fear,
I am the conqueror of darkness.
I am bravery.

Matthew Stewart (12)
The Oratory School

Don't Ask Me

Don't ask me
Who won the cricket,
I'm not bothered about sport.

Don't ask me
Who painted 'The Starry Starry Night',
I don't care for art.

Don't ask me
Who wrote 'The Four Seasons',
Music doesn't move me.

Don't ask me
Who started World War I,
Doesn't mean anything to me.

Don't ask me
Who murdered Martin Luther King,
I couldn't care less.

Don't ask me
Who won the Nobel Prize For Science,
I'm not paid for that.

Don't ask me!
I have no time for silly things,
I've got work to do,
Children to feed,
The rest don't meet my needs.

Samuel Borg (13)
The Oratory School

My Sun

I awoke one morning to a terrible din,
A sun was stuck inside my bin,
I cautiously crept towards the site,
Until it rocked and I leapt back in fright.

The sun put up a tremendous struggle,
I put it down in a crumpled huddle.
This was an extremely evil sun,
So I fed it bad dreams one by one.

After a month I had an uncontrollable sun,
It had eaten my sister and even my mum!
The time had come to get rid of this unholy beast
So I set him a massive feast.

It ate until it was six times as big,
It could not eat even one tiny fig.
When I heard the strain I knew something was wrong,
It exploded with a *splat* and a *bong*.

That was the end of my evil friend,
I hope he will rest from now to the end.

William van der Lande (14)
The Oratory School

An Animal

Prehistoric critter
Swamp ruler
Pool rocker
Big snapper
Log floater
Danger master
Man eater
Green monster.
Alligator!

Ry Moyse (11)
The Oratory School

The Talking Monkey

Back home after school,
I heard noises from the pool,
Rushing down the stairs,
I found a trail of hairs.

Into the pool room I dashed,
On the floor, a mirror smashed,
The fridge was open to my great surprise,
Upon the floor were my grandpa's pies.

Then the moment I'd waited for,
What creature had made the mess on the floor?
Was it a cat, dog, or donkey?
No, a stupid monkey.

It was dancing in the shallow end,
Then swimming from end to end,
Then to my horror it said suddenly,
'Get your trunks and swim with me.'

Believe it or not, the monkey had spoke,
Next he asked for a Diet Coke.
Finally, I fainted on the floor,
Not believing what I saw.

As years passed the monkey lived with me,
It lived off magic bananas and tea,
And to this very day,
The monkey always has something to say.

Oliver Woodward (13)
The Oratory School

Liberté

Don't cry for me when you are down,
I'm in the winds all around.
I'm in the treetops way up high,
I'm in the clouds, in the sky.

Don't mourn for me when you are lonely,
I'm in the grass, the sand, the sea,
I'm always there to help you through things,
I'll be there to see your wedding.

Don't grieve for me when you are doleful,
I'm by your side when you feel sorrowful.
I come to you during your sleep,
It hurts my heart to see you weep.

Don't lament over me when you are low,
I'm in the rain and flakes of snow.
I'm in the tweet of birds in trees,
I was once on Earth but now I'm free.

Alex Bevan (13)
The Oratory School

Luck

I am Luck
I am an Irish shamrock.
The small leprechaun
In my green suit standing tall and proud.
I am the two pence coin
That you find on the street.
I am a wishing well.
Throw in that coin
And it could all come true.

Josh Radley (12)
The Oratory School

Thought!

I am thought,
All day I am around,
Always busy and occupied.
Wondering what to move,
And more importantly where to move.

What's the answer to the sum?
Whom can I ask for help?
Why can I not answer?
All these whos and whats, whys, whens and wheres.

I am mixed up;
I am confused.
I am full of imagination,
Full of words and pieces that don't quite fit together.
I am thought.

Henry Fairbairn (12)
The Oratory School

Defeat

I am defeat.
Every second counts,
Watching, seeing the bails fly off,
Groping in the air as the ball falls down
Into the soft hands,
Trying, but not succeeding.
The laughs of happiness,
The long faces.
Our team has not won.
The bat swings back.
The last batsman has just got out,
Opponents crying with laughter.
Their game has been won.

Edward Stroker (12)
The Oratory School

Life Under The Sea

In the hidden world
Deep under the sea
All the fish can go
Through cities, just like me.

Towns of rock and coral
Villages of weed
All the houses are made
For the fishes' needs.

The bull shark it is vicious
Attacks all that it meets
And while the fish are resting
The catfish cleans the streets.

The parrotfish recycles
The whale is the plane
It takes small fish on holiday
To Ireland or to Spain.

There are the famous killers
Like Billy the Squid Kid
He features in the adult films
So they know what he did.

In the hidden world
Deep under the sea
All the fish can go
Through cities, just like me.

Christopher Armour (13)
The Oratory School

Autumn

Leaves falling to the ground,
Autumn is coming, without a sound.
Squirrels scurry up the trees,
Their movement implies terrible glee.
Conkers fall, golden chestnut halls,
Compared with this my life seems small.
My mind springs open, what a wonderful place,
I walk around leaving hardly a trace.

My mind floats up in the clouds,
All the colours blur together in shrouds,
Purple, green, red, orange and others,
Little boys play, watched by their mothers.
A carpet of leaves beckons before me,
A golden hall will lead me surely.
The birds singing and chirping, here and there,
Clouds swishing and swirling without a care.
Leaves falling to the ground,
Autumn is coming, without a sound.

Matthew Lo (13)
The Oratory School

Bravery And Fear

I am fear,
I am fear in a soldier's eyes,
I am the creak in an attic floor
I am the spider on a murky floor,
I am the fear in a deep dark wood,
I am the never dying fear.

I am bravery,
I stand out among the weak,
I give courage when there is only fear,
I help the wounded in the line of fire,
I am bravery.

Chris Holliss (12)
The Oratory School

The Evil Clock

I found a clock under my bed,
It talked and said it wanted me dead.
Then I hit it with a hammer,
So startled by its manner.

It started ringing very loud,
And out of it rose hissing clouds,
With my air gun I shot the ten,
Shot bounced off and started again.

Then the clock flew at my head,
And I thought, *soon I'll be dead!*
I ducked under the incoming thing,
And it hit the wall with a loud ring.

I closed the window and the door,
Then I realised what locks were for.
I ran back and locked the clock in,
And it got up with a loud ring.

Listen now to my plea for help,
Inside the room I hear it yelp.
I can't hold it much longer in,
Inside I hear a loud *ring ring.*

Sam Smith (13)
The Oratory School

A Kenning

Tree climber
Green skin wearer
Agile jumper
Insect catcher
Poisonous killer
Bug eater
Branch crawler
Amazing creature:
Tree frog

Nicholas Batty (11)
The Oratory School

The Perfect Dream

I dreamt of a place
Far away in a case.
I wonder where it could be?
It's definitely further than the eye can see.

I need to find this land,
Cos I'm starting my new brand.
I'll sell good thoughts and dreams,
I know what I'll sell - rivers and streams.

I wonder who will buy my dream?
Maybe a king or queen who's highly supreme
Or a witch or wizard who needs some more space
Because of the tasks they have to face.

The things I sell are perfectly good quality,
So anyone who comes hasn't got any priority.
Because this land is now basically mine,
Cos I was the one who dreamt it so fine.

I'm leaving my land because I have to wake up,
I would like my tea in my very special cup.
Then I need to get dressed into my clothes
Because I'm going to watch some football pros.

Richard Mark Turner (11)
The Oratory School

Guess What?

Big killer
Great hider
Excellent finder
Heat seeker
Outstanding catcher
Skin shedder
Poison spitter
Mega hunter
Sidewinder
Rattlesnake!

Akumbuom Tihngang (11)
The Oratory School

The Prey Of The Cat

Through the bushes, brushing past the leaves,
Jet-black, stalking what it sees.
Hidden in the bushes, almost invisible,
There lies a jet-black cat,
Crouching down and ready to pounce
And when it does it'll land on the mouse
And maul it in its mouth.

The time has come now that the prey draws nearer,
Not knowing that the cat is there,
Not knowing that its death is near, it carries on eating.

The cat leans back ready to spring,
And its mouth starts to water like a tap.
The cat leaps out like a black streak of lightning.
The prey starts squealing higher than an eagle
Then slowly the prey dies.

Charlie Kopec (11)
The Oratory School

I Am

I am determination.
I complete the easy and the difficult.
I overcome the impossible.
I climb to the top of the highest mountain.
I get to the try line.
I am the only hope.
I am the scorer of the winning goal.
I go, I see, I conquer.

I am capitulation,
I settle for second best.
I go where the wind carries me.
I settle at the back.
I watch the others win.
I am nothing.

Max Canwell (12)
The Oratory School

The Monster

There's something that lurks in the deep undergrowth,
It thrashes around like a mad bull.
Though some people think it's horrible and could do the most
Terrible things but it is very dangerous in many ways.

It is frightening with its big fiery eyes,
Also its vicious, piercing teeth.
If it got let out
Who knows what kind of trouble it could cause?

The monster is about twelve feet tall,
It has the strength of at least one hundred men.
An old man once said that it had been let out before
But there is no stopping it from coming back up from
The dungeon again.

This creature is unlike any other thing on this planet.
Every three hundred years it gets to eat.
Then suddenly it makes it way quickly to the Earth
Destroying everything it possibly can.
The old man cried, 'There is nothing we can do. It is the end!'

Alexander Willis (11)
The Oratory School

A Kenning

Curly tailer,
Pointy earer,
Soft coater,
Human lover,
Viking elder,
Company keeper,
Elk hunter,
Person licker.
Elkhound.

Hugo Lau (11)
The Oratory School

If I Was A Bird

If I was a bird,
I would fly up a million miles
And to places the human eye has never seen before.

I would fly to places far and near,
Such as the park or round the stars,
I would build my nest up high,
So no predator would eat me when they pass by.

I would fly up to the moon as if I were a rocket,
I would go popping all the balloons that greet me
Up high in the sky.

I would go hunting all day long for food for me and my young.
I would scavenge through bins and pick all the fruit off the trees.

I would steal the seeds that the farmers had laid down for me.
But I would not be scared of the scarecrow as I would know it
Was not real and just stuffed.

Charles Portwain (11)
The Oratory School

The Hunt

As me and the other hounds closed in with haste
We'll have caught that fox by the end of the chase.
The adrenaline pumped as we raged ever faster
And faintly in the distance I hear the call of my master.
I love every moment, the thrill of the chase
And on and on and on we'll race
Until we have caught that fox but now we must run
Until I hear the sound of my master's gun.
There he goes first left then right,
We have confused him you see, this should give him a fright.
I have jumped up upon his back
I snap at his neck and for him all is black.

Freddie Dash (11)
The Oratory School

I Am

I am fear.
I make the bravest of men quiver.
I make veterans of war drop their guns and surrender to the enemy.
I cast a dark shadow over the world.

I am bravery.
I am the bold knight on a long journey to slay a dragon.
I am a courageous leader standing proud.
I am the fireman who dares to enter the building.

Michael Phipps (12)
The Oratory School

Revenge

I am revenge

    I cause wars and brew hate between nations.
    I stand proud in the group of the seven deadly sins.
    I cause death, hate, envy and greed.
    I never settle for less, I cannot compromise.
    I cannot lose, even if it means worldwide destruction.

I am revenge

Tom Barker (12)
The Oratory School

Hate

I am hate,
    I bring destruction and fear to the world.
    I am the gun at war and the punch in a fight.
    I bring despair and sorrow to the world.
    I make blood, pain and death.
    I am the lost tooth from a fight, the biased referee.
    I am the hilltop fort and the three-forked trident.
        I am hate.

Andrew Mudge (13)
The Oratory School

The Meadow

The meadow is as gloomy as a swamp,
The meadow is sited high in the hills,
The meadow is as boggy as a swamp,
The meadow is as dark as night,
The meadow watches just like a hawk,
The meadow doesn't let anyone enter,
The meadow will lash out at anything that enters,
The meadow is always there and once in you're never let out,
The meadow is like a maze, if you get lost you'll never see light again,
The meadow is a never-ending world of doom,
The meadow is like a living creature,
The meadow is as dull as can be,
The meadow is a living nightmare you can't beat,
The meadow can tell if there is something near,
The meadow cares about nothing but itself,
The meadow wipes out anything in its way, like a nuclear bomb,
The meadow scours the area just like a fox,
The meadow will always be waiting no matter where you are.

Thomas Brimacombe (11)
The Oratory School

Death

Death is knocking on my door,
It's coming for me, it's coming.
I'm hiding in the corner but it's coming for me.
I'm running, heart beating, feet smacking, but it's coming for me.
I can't escape.
I think of my mother and father, but it's coming.
It's dark, it's wet and I'm scared.
It's drifting, floating, coming . . .
I'm getting a stitch, I stop and jog backwards into an alley.
I turn around and bump into it.
I spin again but it's there with its hood and its scythe.
Then I wake up, I am hot and sweaty and the window is open
And there's a knock on my door . . .

Julian Jest (11)
The Oratory School

Dragon Dream

If I was a dragon . . .

If I was a dragon, I would want to be a king or a god dragon.
If I was a king dragon, I would want to have world travel.
If I was a god dragon, I would want to have many, many Christians.

I am the king dragon and I go to . . .

When I go to China, I change my body to a boy's
And I play many, many things in the games centre.
When I go to Korea, I change my body to a man's body
And I eat many, many things in the restaurants.

I am the god dragon . . .

If I can go to other planets then I will go.
After five days and I find another planet, I will give it a name
The name will be Yochiarth I want to live here but there are giants here.
I try to defeat them but they are too strong.
I make plans to move them away from the planet.

The giants move away and now I live here on this planet.

Yochi Nakamura (11)
The Oratory School

Hate And Love

I am hate. I am another god.
I can create wars and end lives.
I can ruin friendships.
I can turn a good soul into a monster.
I can bring out pure evil and make people do foolish things.
I can damage lives by making revenge feel good.

I am love. I bring happiness to the world.
I make people care and protect each other.
I bring couples together for the rest of their lives.

Jamie Lyons (12)
The Oratory School

A Dog's Life

Creak! The noise came from the stair
Someone was coming, I jumped off the chair.
I ran to my bed and started to snore
To make out that I'd been there all night before.

'Come on Buster! Get up!' she said
So I waddled slowly from my bed.
She dished up my favourite Pedigree Chum
I gobbled it up adding more to my big tum.

'Walkies!' she shouted, so to the door I ran
I love to get out and chase that man!
You know the one who delivers post
He's the one I like to get the most.

Back home again, ready for my sleep
Walking can make a dog tired so in I creep.
Into my bed, I flop down with a thwack
And dream of men in uniform carrying sacks.

James Chaplin (11)
The Oratory School

Fear

I am fear

> I am fear on both sides of the battlefield
> I am fear in the steps the enemy takes
> I am fear as the first cannon ball hits the ground
> I am fear as the next man hits the cold, unforgiving ground
> I am fear as my soldiers take another innocent life
> I am fear as we lift our swords for victory

I am fear

Nick Polkinghorne (12)
The Oratory School

Guess What?

Anything eater
Muddy roller
Podgy porker
Loud grunter
Slow mover
Not clever
Load grinder
A pig!

Duncan James (11)
The Oratory School

Guess Who?

Fast runner
Muscle builder
Amazing power
England's winner
Great starter
Crowd stunner
Gets hotter
Dwayne Chambers!

Jamie Radnedge (11)
The Oratory School

A Kenning

Keen predator
Golden soarer
Prey hunter
Pretty featherer
Scottish dweller
Nest builder
Chick bearer
Piercing crier.
Golden eagle!

Alasdair Brown (11)
The Oratory School

The Mystery Creature

Hairy creature
People hunter
Fly eater
Creepy crawler
Mini beaster
Tiny scarer
Eight legger
Web spinner
Very clever
Quick mover.
A spider!

Nicholas Ansell (11)
The Oratory School

Guess Who?

England kit wearer
Everton player
Skilled kicker
Magnificent striker
Famous youngster
Talented scorer
Fast runner
Arsenal beater.
Wayne Rooney!

Simon Allan (11)
The Oratory School